Selling Vegetables to Drunks

Lessons I Learned as an Alcoholic's Daughter

Praise for Selling Vegetables to Drunks

"Laurie Hellmann fearlessly illuminates the challenging terrain of childhood trauma with a rare blend of empathy, expertise, and profound insight. This book is not just a guide; it is a beacon of hope for anyone navigating the complexities of their past."
Allison Luallen - *Friend of the Author*

"Honest, courageous, and inspirational. A must-read for anyone wishing to be uplifted and encouraged to be a better human from the challenges we inherited and encountered from our childhood experiences and throughout our lives. My childhood ran parallel to the childhood memories shared by the author regarding her father who had alcohol and smoking addictions and the challenges it raised. The author chose to use these challenges she encountered to grow, not repeat the cycles from her father, and make better lives for herself, her husband, and her children."
Karen Roberts - *Retired Lieutenant in Law Enforcement Emotional Intelligence Training Facilitator*

"Despite the raw subject matter requiring her self-awareness and vulnerability, I found this to be a very enjoyable read! Laurie has a writing style that really draws you in and makes you feel like you are 'riding shotgun' on her personal journey. While I can't fully fathom her relationship with her deceased father, I can applaud and attest to the fact that she is an incredible mother, despite the lack of role models in her own childhood."
Sandy Lamb - *CEO, Altitude Executive Coaching (Colorado Springs, CO)*

"Told with the candor and vulnerability that is her trademark, Hellmann's second memoir recounts the origin story of a true survivor and warrior mom. *Selling Vegetables to Drunks* is a compelling story full of heart and humor as a mother/daughter road trip becomes an opportunity to explore and exorcise demons that plagued the author's childhood."
Joanna Monahan - *Award-winning Author of* Something Better

"Reading *Selling Vegetables to Drunks* felt like stepping into a mirror and seeing my own childhood reflected back at me. Laurie's raw and unfiltered recounting of her upbringing, marred by the chaos and pain of living with an alcoholic parent, resonates deeply with those who have walked a similar path. Her courage to bare the darkest corners of her past, coupled with her determination to break the cycle of abuse and addiction, is nothing short of inspiring. As a fellow autism parent and forever caregiver, our shared experience of navigating uncharted and often overwhelming terrain adds another layer of connection to her story. This book is a must-read for anyone who has felt the sting of addiction and for those who strive to create a better future for their own children despite the burdens of their past. Laurie's story is not just about survival; it's about triumph and finding purpose in pain."
Shannon Urquiola - *Owner and Founder, Not Your Average Autism Mom*

"Laurie Hellmann's journey is a testament to the human spirit's incredible resilience. Her bravery in confronting her past and sharing her story inspires us to face our challenges head-on. Her raw and honest narrative shows that every moment of adversity has a purpose, offering hope and strength to those who read her words. *Selling Vegetables to Drunks* offers a profound exploration of the spiritual journey that transforms pain into purpose. Hellmann masterfully depicts how our struggles are not just random occurrences, but divine preparations for greater service and understanding. This book is an inspiring guide for anyone seeking to find meaning in their suffering and embrace their true calling."

Laura Leaton Roberts, MEd, PCC - *Executive Coach and Leadership Trainer*

"This inspiring memoir is an honest, searing, and sometimes heartbreaking portrayal of author Laurie Hellmann's life. As she courageously exposes her secretive childhood, which was filled with emotional abuse from her alcoholic father, she realizes how this early adversity prepared her for successfully navigating a challenging motherhood experience. This realization freed Laurie from mental obstacles she harbored for many years and put her on the path to healing and ultimately to learning to savor the joys in her life. Anyone who has experienced hardships, especially in their childhood, will be motivated to see them as potential gifts that can transform a life of resentment into a life of contentment."

Feef Dillon - *Friend of the Author and Member of the Marshall Historical Society (Marshall, MI)*

"I have known Laurie for many years and watched her navigate her world with confidence, beauty, and grace, always with a smile on her face. Laurie has been and continues to be very talented, excelling in everything she attempts. She always has had many friends, and outside her home, she presented a very positive image at every stage of development. I knew differently. When you looked in her eyes, they told another story. Laurie's book, *Selling Vegetables to Drunks*, is beautifully constructed and executed as it provides her reader with valuable insights into a home riddled with all the complex emotions, experiences, roles, and interactions that take place in an abusive family. *Selling Vegetables to Drunks* is a very powerful read, in which Laurie examines her life and takes us on a journey where we all learn more about abuse and how it impacts everyone. Through deep self-reflection, Laurie has processed and learned from all her life's relationships (positive and negative) to find her own path of love and acceptance. This book is for all of us who work toward compassion and open communication in our relationships."

Candice Putnam - *Director of Adult and Community Education and Elementary Principal (Retired), Marshall Public Schools*

"Laurie Hellmann's *Selling Vegetables to Drunks* is everything I had hoped it would be — unique but relatable, raw but uplifting, conversational but introspective. It is a book that is everything all at once, and effortlessly and poetically so — a book that is seated in the possibilities and promise of today but rooted in the stark realities of a dysfunctional and painful past. As a reader, I felt a connection to the innocent and impressionable child Laurie once was and the grounded adult — and loving, devoted parent — she has become. A powerful and entertaining memoir for a broad audience of readers and an especially important book for those who have emerged from childhood darkness, ready to forgive and grow after a lifetime of living in the shadow of their loved one's addiction."

Kate Colbert - *Business Author, Poet, Executive Coach, Higher-Education Expert, Marketer, Healthcare Advocate, and Former Wife of an Alcoholic*

"Stories left untold and buried in our souls are revealed and dealt with in this book. Having known Laurie in her high school days through dance and soccer, she always had an especially beautiful warm smile and demeanor. Laurie stood out well above the crowd in her contemporary hip-hop clogging, where her spirit shone through! She was the inspiration for other dancers, including our daughter. Little did most of us know of the challenges she was facing at home with her father's abusive words and actions. Instead of falling into the path of destruction, she embraced the lessons and transformed them into being the best she could be.

Laurie continues to let her brilliant light shine through the darkness. I have always seen (and still see) that magical light that she mustered up on stage. I'm so thankful that she can share that light with the world through her books and blogs. Through her writing, Laurie shows us the path to understanding and caring for others in similar situations. Like her first book, this is another must-read."

Sue Rosko - *Speech-language Pathologist and Educator, Child Advocate, and Longtime Admirer of the Author*

"Laurie Hellmann takes us where few dare to go — the past. Unflinching and honest in the pages of *Selling Vegetables to Drunks*, she tells her story about a chaotic childhood and the imprint it leaves on her, long into adulthood. There is a piece of all of us in her narrative. Her words will break you open and heal you at the exact same time."

Carrie Cariello - *Writer, Blogger, and Autism Advocate*

"From the very first page, *Selling Vegetables to Drunks* captivates with its raw honesty and powerful storytelling. This remarkable memoir chronicles the life of an extraordinary woman who transforms the trials of her tumultuous childhood into a fierce commitment to her children. Growing up with an abusive, alcoholic father, she learned early the strength required to survive and the courage to protect those she loves.

Her journey from a childhood marked by fear and instability — to becoming a champion for her children, including a nonspeaking autistic child — is nothing short of inspirational. Every chapter is a testament to her resilience, showing how the scars of her past became the armor she needed to advocate for her children in a world that often misunderstands and over-looks their needs.

This memoir is more than a story — it's a beacon of hope for parents and caregivers every-where. It's a celebration of the indomitable human spirit and a powerful reminder that our past does not define us — it prepares us for the battles we must fight and the love we must give. A must-read for anyone seeking inspiration and a deeper understanding of a mother's unwavering dedication."

Dawnmarie Gaivin, RN, BSN - *Spellers Method Cofounder and Mom of Two Nonspeakers*

"Laurie's exploration of her 'fissured and bumpy memory lane' of childhood trauma is a profound odyssey of self-reflection and emotional upheaval. This introspective journey — one that many of us ought to embark upon — delves into the depths of personal growth often shunned and obscured in the recesses of our minds. Her candid discussion of family abuse and neglect, and its replacement with love and acceptance in her own life, delivers a truly powerful message of hope and guidance for anyone seeking to transform their own lives."

Max Peel - *Tour Leader for Intrepid Travel, ARK Disability Services Staff Member, and Zoology/Ecology Student at JCU Australia*

Selling Vegetables to Drunks

Lessons I Learned as an Alcoholic's Daughter

Laurie L. Hellmann

Endless Charades
Publishing

Selling Vegetables to Drunks
Lessons I Learned as an Alcoholic's Daughter

Copyright 2024 by Laurie L. Hellmann

Published by Endless Charades Publishing (Aurora, CO)

Editing by:
Beth Rayner & Kate Colbert

Cover design and typesetting by:
Spiro Books

First edition: September 2024

Paperback ISBN: 979-8-9910758-0-0
Jacketed Hard Cover ISBN: 979-8-9910758-1-7
Hard Cover ISBN: 979-8-9910758-2-4

Library of Congress Control Number: 2024915682

The stories and details shared in this book are complete and accurate to the author's best recollection.

Content Warning

Please be advised that *Selling Vegetables to Drunks* contains stories about domestic violence, mental and emotional abuse, child neglect, and addiction, which might be difficult or deeply personal to some readers. Readers feeling suicidal, experiencing suicidal ideation, or having thoughts of hurting themselves should call the National Suicide Prevention Hotline at 1-800-273-TALK (8255) or visit SuicidePreventionLifeline.org. Readers affected by addiction: Know there is help and there is hope. Treatment options vary, state by state. Treat yourself with love and compassion by connecting with local resources.

Dedication

To my children, Kendall and Skyler, for loving
me through my parenting mistakes.

To my sister Beth, for protecting me, supporting
me, and ultimately helping me to heal.

And to all survivors of family-member addiction — may you find peace
and strength, and a life free from chaos and fear. It's not your fault.

Contents

Preface
By Laurie L. Hellmann.. xv

Foreword
By Beth Rayner.. xxi

Dead End:
Finding Out My Father Died 1

The Ride Home:
Conversations With My Daughter 8

A Bumpy Road:
Learning Patience The Hard Way 13

3-Point Turn:
Seeking Validation, Strength and Confidence............................. 29

Buckle Up:
Releasing Our Secrets.. 44

Cruising:
A Tour Through My Past.. 55

Hazard Lights:
Ignoring What Hurts 64

Body Shop:
Confronting Our Generational Trauma....................................... 74

Rear View Mirror:
The Truth About Where I Come From.. 82

Drive In:
Family Bonding as We Grieve 87

Hitting the Brakes:
Too Little, Too Late... 97

A Fork in the Road:
From Abuse to Abandonment 105

Tank on Empty:
My Struggles with Affection 120

Tinted Windows:
Perspective and Perception 130

New Lease:
Life After Death... 138

Epilogue.. 145
My Life in Pictures... 155
Acknowledgments... 165
Go Beyond the Book.. 168
About the Author.. 170

Preface

By Laurie L. Hellmann

Here we go again — commemorating another book and another chance to meet you, my reader, in a truly honest, raw, vulnerable, and complete way. Thank you for this opportunity — for being here with me when it's scary. I am ready (finally!) and I hope you are ready too. I entitled my first book Welcome to My Life and, right now, in this second book, I'd like to welcome you to my family. In the pages that follow, you'll meet them all: my mother and father, my sister, aunts and uncles, two husbands (for worse and for better), and my two spectacular children, Skyler and Kendall. While my parenting journey has been periodically bumpy — often requiring that I navigate uncharted, unrelatable terrain — I have come to understand that my own transition from being someone's child to being some children's mother has taken me on a purposeful journey to who I was meant to be. Motherhood is the teaching tool that has guided (and healed) my life; being a mom (sometimes under overwhelming circumstances) has offered me the chance to take on the most important role I didn't realize I needed. It is a role and an opportunity that God had prepared me for all along.

As you are about to learn, my childhood wasn't all popsicles and bedtime stories. It was rough, complicated, and painful. It forced me to grow up too fast, to confront big emotions like fear and shame, and to craft an adult life that simultaneously ran far, far away while never quite being able to escape where I had been. I've had career success and personal growth, but none of it helped me heal from my own childhood. It was the miraculous journey of becoming a mother — and slaying my own demons in service to my children — that has presented me with the op-portunity to rewrite my story, using all that I'd learned (the hard way) as fuel to provide my children with the safe, loving childhood that was withheld from me. I always promised myself that no matter what my motherhood journey brought with it, I would break the cycle of abuse and addiction that had plagued my family for generations. It would end with me. Banned from my home would be the harsh words and stinging criticisms that leave wounds of self-doubt and internal suffering not easily or quickly healed. Those words, those looks, those behaviors, those raised voices and raised eyebrows — they can brand us emotionally to a depth that controls your every thought, action, and opinion through the entirety of your life ... unless you're willing to acknowledge it and work to release it. *I would do better*, I promised myself and my children. The kinds of rage and impatience that characterized my youth would be replaced with the emotional and physical connection that was significantly lacking throughout my childhood. I was going to give my children everything I had needed and not received. I was not going to "live vicariously" through them, as far too many parents do, but I was going to *heal* through them as they were nurtured into their best selves, safe to be whoever they were destined to be.

I was committed to showing up differently as a parent — to giving my kids the childhood of my dashed and deferred dreams and to providing them with the kind of formative years they wouldn't have to seek therapy to recover from.

All parents, despite their best efforts, pass on both good and unde-sirable traits to their children. But some parents fall far, far short on ex-hibiting "best efforts." Some show up, just barely, to this odyssey we call "parenthood." I was raised in a home with addiction at the forefront. My sister, my mom, and I were too busy swimming in alcohol and cruelty — just trying to keep our heads above water from day to day as the children and spouse of one of the town drunks — to get any positive takeaways from family life. Looking back, I don't see the "lessons," "values," or even traditions that I hear other people talk about when it comes to their upbringings; I just see an overpowering spotlight on the negatives, such as low self-esteem, the practice of denial, poor anger management skills, poor emotional regulation skills, narcissism, passive-aggressive behavior, and possibly the genetic markers for addiction and depression. My childhood was a dark time and, until very recently, I didn't want to talk about it. And to be fair, while both my parents were alive, I didn't feel I *could* talk about it.

We each have a story, and each of our stories matters. But does mine matter *enough* to rock the boat of my immediate and extended family to finally tell the truth — confidently, publicly, and without shame … here, in a book for you? I think it does. So, after years of excuses as to why I should wait to write and publish this memoir, here we are.

I've paused and resumed the drafting of this book many times until my reasons to complete it finally outweighed my reasons to refrain. Sometimes while writing and revisiting the painful events throughout my childhood — moments that I thought had been fully dissected and resolved during years of therapy — I was overcome with an unexpected emotional response. The tears streaming down my face as I typed each disturbing memory in grave detail indicated that those buried feelings and insecurities were alive and well and that I needed to release them to officially move on and enjoy my life.

I have heard the expression "We are only as sick as our secrets," and that struck a chord with me. We all — even those with relatively idyllic childhoods and lives full of fortune and blessings — harbor some sort of secret that we have kept (often for years or decades) out of shame or obligation or fear. I've been keeping secrets my whole life. I was distracted with fear and worry that sharing my story at the wrong time could be damaging to others. I kept telling myself that "once enough time passed" or when the main offender in most of my stories was no longer around ("after my dad dies"), sharing my truth would be easier. I don't know that I'd say it's "easier," but I do feel like it's time. I realize that as I prepare to tell you my story — a story that belongs to many members of my family but that is still very much mine to tell — the words I'm about to say cannot be rescinded. The burden of hurting others through what I reveal to those on the periphery of our family remains a heavy weight on my shoulders.

In the end, there is no such thing as "perfect timing" — only "I feel ready." Through the process of writing and editing this book, I have gained immeasurable clarity and confidence about who I am as an individual, a wife, a sister, a daughter, a friend, and a mother. Parenting Skyler and Kendall while simultaneously acknowledging the little girl inside me has helped me make sense of my childhood and release myself from the negative labels and insecurities that have haunted me my entire life. I am no longer envious of people who have had "easy" childhoods, but instead consider myself stronger and wiser for having overcome mine. I've been offered the opportunity to view the world differently — a world in which God gives you what you *need* instead of what you *want*, as a means of illuminating your ultimate purpose.

In sharing the story of my life, I wish to validate the young child in all of us who may still suffer from low self-esteem or the belief that they can't achieve incredible things because someone in their life programmed them to believe that to be true. More importantly, I want that inner child to understand one of the biggest lessons I've learned: feelings aren't facts. My parenting philosophy is all about feelings, but not the kind of feelings that nearly destroyed me when I was growing up. My primary focus while raising both of my children has been ensuring that I provide them with the basic emotional foundation they deserve from me — validation, affection, and acceptance — while empowering them to live with confidence, never having to feel a single negative thing about themselves. "You worthless piece of …" are words that were said to me but never said to my children. It is my deepest hope that my children feel only positive things about themselves and that the only feelings I "give" them are ones that make them feel worthy, loved, respected, and accepted for precisely who they are.

In every chapter of this book, I endeavor to be transparent and raw, and I refuse to let fear and resentment continue to take up precious real estate in my mind. As you are reading, I hope my work (and the risks I take) in this regard will inspire you to break free of whatever may be holding *you* back from living *your* best life. I believe that our life experiences are always teaching us something — and preparing us for or connecting us to what is yet to come. But it takes a shift in perspective and a big dose of courage to see the true beauty of where we've been or the purposeful life lessons that are borne from our challenges.

Foreword

By Beth Rayner

W hen my sister asked me to write the foreword for this memoir, I wanted it to be an opportunity to validate her truth. Because her truth is my truth, as well.

Together, we experienced the same childhood environment though, admittedly, our memories are slightly different. Each impactful moment affected us uniquely. We tended to accurately reflect the stereotypical roles of the children of alcoholics. I was pretty much the classic "hero" character: Type A, overachieving perfectionist oldest child who is courageous enough to fight back (in my case, usually with sarcasm) and who often faces harsh consequences. Laurie was more of a "peacemaker" who, even as a child, tried to calm the storm, despite being powerless against the raging winds, thunder, and lightning. I fought, and she brokered peace, and in the end, the trajectory of our lives still paralleled in many ways:

- In our individual drives toward achievement.
- In our first marriages to men who we inevitably (and subconsciously) chose so they might help stabilize an internal chaos created by a traumatic childhood.
- In our necessary therapy in our 30s, when we finally acknowledged a level of unhappiness that we each could no longer just smile our way through, pretending everything was fine as we had done our entire lives.
- From the decision to bet on ourselves and divorce our husbands, tapping into an inner strength and resilience that ironically developed *from* our shared childhood trauma.

- And ultimately in our approach to parenting, with a dedicated focus to developing emotional availability and affection, despite never really experiencing either of those things ourselves as children or young adults.

We are more alike than we are different. I am proud to say that.

Because Laurie and I are so close in age (17 months apart) and had only each other to rely on as childhood playmates, dance partners, and teenage girls trying to navigate relationships despite a life of dysfunction, you'd think we would have remained close as we moved into adulthood. But as soon as I graduated from high school, I was hell bent on forging my own path and finally feeling a sense of control when everything I had known until then was controlled by the antics of an alcoholic father and a co-dependent mother. So, I left — not realizing that I'd just contributed to a sense of abandonment that Laurie, the peacemaker, had always felt. We remained distant through much of our 20s, each trying to create successful lives for ourselves on our own terms and each unaware that a lifetime of things unsaid was bubbling under the surface, ready to explode.

For both of us, motherhood was both a trial by fire and a gift from above. I firmly believe that God chose me to be the mother of my beautiful babies, Madeline and William. He trusted me with nurturing them, even though in many respects He knew that I lacked some of the most important qualities and skills to do so. I lacked patience. I was quick to temper. I wasn't physically affectionate. I hated noise. I despised mediocrity, which led to unrealistic expectations of myself and others. But I do have *vision*. Perseverance and grit. Courage. And an innate sense of introspection and self-reflection. So, when Laurie had her first child, a beautiful boy named Skyler, our adult relationship began to grow from the shared experience of parenthood. She, too, struggled to work through impatience, perfectionism, and displays of affection. She, too, was courageous and persevered through adversity. And the seeds for this memoir were planted.

It started with repeated mentions of "remember when" and discussing things we said — back when we were children — that we would *never* do when we became parents. Together, we began remembering what it was like to be parented by our parents, while the experience of *being* parents gave us an opportunity to see it all in a new light. We came to confide in one another that we sometimes struggled against the kneejerk reactions that would have us repeat those patterns. We filled in the gaps of our years apart, talking through overwhelming feelings of guilt that seemed to dominate our choices. We each had a need for validation and approval that seemed to drive our perfectionism, and we acknowledged the inherent conflict avoidance that undermined our strength. And for two people who were accustomed to just keeping things to themselves, we trusted each other enough to share our feelings about who we were and how our divergent paths ended up in parallel.

Like most parents, as our children grew, we entertained them with "back in my day" stories, but most of those stories highlighted dysfunction, and very few had happy endings. Laurie would come "home" to Michigan for a visit, and we'd go together to the bar where our dad was still a permanent fixture, and we'd say hello. It's a small town, and many of our childhood friends still live there, but it was surprising to us that when we'd run into people on these bar trips, most didn't connect the dots and realize Rocky was our dad. And inevitably, we'd find ourselves reliving our adolescence, telling them things they had no idea about back then. We often heard, "Damn, you girls need to write a book."

We have been talking about co-authoring a memoir for years but were always stuck on a theme. It couldn't just be about being children of an alcoholic and the trauma we experienced from that. However, we struggled with what to do with the hurt and heartache. Inevitably, life got in the way, and we sidelined the idea until Laurie decided to write a different memoir, *Welcome to My Life: A Personal Parenting Journey Through Autism.* Throughout the writing process and publication, dozens of speaking engagements, her podcast, and her social media presence, people often asked her how she did it. How did she manage to not only hold it together through the trials and tribulations of raising two children, but with one of those children having significant special needs? Soon after she published her first book, Laurie and I were being interviewed for a podcast hosted by one of Laurie's high-school friends, and Laurie was once again asked this exact question: How did she do it? The conversation that followed connected her resilience throughout her parenting journey to the resilience and strength she developed from our childhood. Everything we experienced back then shaped the mother she has become (and needed to be) for each of her children. Like most people, our friend was shocked by our candid storytelling, having had no idea that would be the direction his "overcoming challenges" podcast would take. And that became the focus of this book.

I am honored to offer the final sentences of introduction before you delve into this remarkable book. Laurie's writing combines storytelling and honest, thoughtful self-reflection. You will be captivated, educated, inspired, and even emotionally exposed. Please "go there" with Laurie — to her deepest pain and most profound purpose. Let this book entertain you and even change you. Let Laurie's stories sit heavily and then lightly upon your heart. Heal with her. She offers us all a rare and poignant opportunity in the pages ahead. Perhaps this book will inspire you to embrace the hardships that you've overcome and seek to better understand yourself in the process. I wish that for you, regardless of your personal situation. For Laurie, working through her past and being grateful for how it influenced her present has strengthened her faith, taught her the power of forgiveness, and empowered her in ways that she never could have imagined.

The lessons she learned as an alcoholic's daughter are lessons from which we can all grow and thrive ... and heal.

Dead End:

Finding Out My Father Died

The morning of October 1, 2020, started out like any other Thursday. At the first beep of the 6:00 a.m. alarm, I jumped out of bed, threw on the workout clothes I had neatly folded and left on the bathroom countertop the night before, brushed my teeth, and made my rounds through the house — feeding animals and packing lunches. The fact that my morning routine doesn't include a piping hot cup of coffee — that my eyes fully open to a new day without the trickery of caffeine — shocks most people. Truth be told, I have never liked coffee; I love the smell but just cannot stand the taste.

It was 2020 and, like most of the world adjusting to a pandemic "new normal," my husband and I were both working from home. He was already awake and responding to company emails. I hadn't gotten that far yet because serving as the "school bus" that day was my unofficial job before I started my paying job. The oven clock flashed 7:15 a.m. (*hadn't it just been 6 o'clock?!*) and knowing that all hell would break loose if we didn't stick to our tight schedule, I instinctively hollered, "We need to hit the road, Kendall!" to my daughter. She is anything but a morning person and tends to move at a snail's pace. Maybe *she* needs some coffee! After all these years, I'm convinced she dawdles simply because it annoys her mother.

Doing my best to keep my cool and keep smiling, I feverishly gathered overflowing backpacks and hurried the kids out the door, mentally preparing myself for the impending nightmare that is my daughter's high school drop-off and pick-up line. I have never been in a rush for her to grow up, but damn if those annoying traffic patterns in the school parking lot — specifically dictated by orange cones and teachers waving parents along — didn't make me eager for the day when I could avoid this chaos when she became a licensed driver and took *herself* to school. After practically shoving her from my moving vehicle to avoid violating the policy against "lingering" in the line for more than 1.5 minutes, I veered my car back toward the highway and proceeded to the adjacent town, where my son attends an autism therapy center.

At 17 years old, Skyler should be in the same high school with his sister; however, due to his nonspeaking autism diagnosis and profound needs, going to school with his sister was never an option. The autism therapy center is the most appropriate place for him to receive the critical support and resources that traditional schools in our area are not equipped to provide.

Skyler's drop-off that day was uneventful, and I continued home. Dropping my keys on the kitchen counter around 8:15 a.m., I moved to the next thing on my extremely structured day's agenda. This was the point in the morning when I would typically go for a run or ride the Peloton bike. I know that by dressing for exercise the moment I wake up and going into autopilot with a pre-planned workout the minute I return home from my chauffeuring duties, I am less likely to become distracted with work and lose the only guaranteed "me time" that I get.

I have always been the type of person who thrives on consistency and lists, never comfortable with spontaneity or winging it. In fact, lack of planning, preparation, or control heightens my anxiety. I'm not a fan. So, on this day, without hesitation, I strapped on my cycling shoes and logged into the 45-minute hip hop-themed Peloton ride I had selected the night before. I had a tried-and-true plan and a proven approach to tackling my morning. It worked for me, and I worked for it. As the final seconds of the class ticked down, my mind instantly shifted to work mode, sifting through the lengthy to-do list required of me as a leader and coach of 25 salespeople. I unclipped my shoes from the bike pedals and, while beginning a quick stretch, I heard the vibration of my cell phone in the plastic cup holder of the bike's handlebars. I glanced at the glowing screen, and the sight of the caller's name caused the little hairs on my neck to stand up. As I quickly grabbed the phone to answer, my stomach churned, and my mind reeled with unsettling thoughts.

Had he been admitted to the hospital yet again?

Had he finally succumbed to the years of self-inflicted damage on his body ... and died?

Although I had mentally prepared for the latter scenario, it's hard to really know how you might feel or react when receiving the news.

The familiar female voice on the other end, my Aunt Nancy, spoke with a calm but serious tone. "Rocky passed away this morning," she said. My heart dropped. I stood there, frozen, in complete silence. It was as if all the things that I thought were important only moments prior no longer mattered. On the one hand, I was relieved because it was finally over - his suffering and mine; he could no longer disappoint me. My relief immediately turned to guilt. *Why am I not upset? He's my father, yet I don't feel instant grief or sadness.* After what felt like an eternity, I said the only words I could think to say at that moment: "Wow, just three days shy of his 72nd birthday." I asked a few additional questions about his passing and, as we ended the call, she promised to keep me apprised of the funeral arrangements and further details as she learned them.

I can't remember whether I set my phone down or gripped it absent-mindedly as I ran upstairs but I know that in the wake of that call, it felt nuclear. My dad was dead.

Unable to process the news fully, I immediately went into business mode and made a mental list of people I needed to call — people who my aunt hadn't yet spoken to. My obvious first call was to my sister. Knowing she was in the middle of teaching her 6th grade Reading class, I texted her with an urgent message to call me back as soon as possible. I waited for her to respond before I shared the news with anyone else. Moments after my text, she called and said, "Did Dad die? Because I know you would only interrupt me during the school day if it was serious." Her reaction was the same as mine: matter of fact and interested mostly in future details. We only spoke for a few minutes, and I told her I would call our mom.

I hung up with my sister, took a deep breath and dialed my mom — having absolutely no idea what her reaction would be. When she answered, I jumped right into it, "Rocky died." She gasped, "Oh Laurie, I'm so sorry to hear that." Her voice cracked as she choked back tears, "How are you doing?" I assured her I was okay and agreed to keep her updated. Shocked by her emotional response to the death of her abusive ex-husband, and to keep from triggering my own emotions, I abruptly ended the conversation by explaining that I had many more people to contact.

I now had the uncomfortable obligation of reaching out to inform close and distant friends and relatives of my father's death. As harsh as it may sound, with each number dialed, I braced myself for the varied responses I would surely get. Some people broke down into tears and others maintained their composure, simply asking me to keep them updated on the plans for the service. I had no idea which of my own emotions to express so I could meet the moment of their responses. I stuck to the facts as I understood them and let them lead the way with their words or tears, or lack thereof.

After experiencing the grief of others, I started to feel the deep sadness that I was missing before. I was sad that a life had ended, sad for the many buried emotions and unspoken words now left permanently unsaid, and sad for the lost opportunity to finally understand one another.

I had envisioned this day many times over the years, and in none of those reflections did I shed a single tear over the thought of him dying. That may sound extremely cold, but I carried so much anger and resentment for my father that concerning myself with his wellbeing was not even a footnote on my priority list. I never imagined having much empathy for him and I surely never thought I'd be heartbroken by losing him. For my entire adult life, I was completely numb when it came to my feelings for my dad — I genuinely believed I had released myself of any emotional connection to him. So, it was deeply confusing to me when I burst into tears following my final "death notice" phone call that day. Why the sudden waterworks?

My husband, Josh, having heard bits and pieces of my conversations, came up from his makeshift office in our basement to inquire about what was going on. I instantly lunged into him for a reassuring hug and shared the details.

"Oh no, I'm so sorry. Are you okay?" he responded, clearly concerned.

"I think so," I said, voice shaking. "I mean, I knew it was likely coming, but it's just hard to prepare for how it will feel, how to process the roller coaster of emotions. You know?"

Josh is an emotional, careful, thoughtful, spiritually grounded person, so the question he posed next was typically insightful and gave me a sense of intense clarity.

"Do you think you are sad at the thought of never getting the closure you wanted and needed? Are you okay with never getting an apology or explanation?"

I had not really put my finger on it, but as soon as he said it, I realized that was exactly it. Death is final, and we take all our secrets and unresolved feelings with us when we depart this life — leaving those we have wronged to pick up the pieces and to struggle with how to make sense of it all. I was angry. And I was sad that the anger had nowhere to go.

I had so many thoughts and questions, but I particularly wrestled with God's timing. Why had my father's death occurred now? Over the past five years, he had multiple hospitalizations for a broken hip, a heart attack (requiring CPR on the floor of the bar to revive him), and breathing issues due to COPD caused by 50+ years of smoking. One such ambulance ride and hospital admission resulted in a lengthy, medically induced coma which prompted our Catholic family to bring in a priest to administer last rites and instruct those at his bedside to say our goodbyes. But with each near-death experience, my dad awoke — against all odds — and swiftly returned to his corner bar stool to live an unaltered, empty life. His existence was full only inasmuch as it was overflowing with alcohol and tobacco in almost mind-blowing excess.

Nearly dead, time after time, my dad had become a sort of fabled "survivor." Nothing kept him down for long. But now, it was over.

In the early moments after learning my dad had died, I found myself thinking about those multiple near-death experiences and wondering why I had continually hung onto the expectation that nearly dying would inspire him to change. I had a naïve, unfounded faith in him because I had that kind of faith in humanity. Aren't people supposed to bounce back better — and make something of themselves — after they hit "rock bottom?" I often wondered why he could never appreciate or accept that he was repeatedly given the gift of more time — why he didn't use that blessing (that second chance!) to make amends to those he had harmed. Perhaps his shame was just too overwhelming, and maybe he didn't know how or where to begin. That's what I like to think, anyway. Believing that he *purposely* chose to give no apologies or explanations for his behavior (to me, my sister, my mom, and others) while on this Earth — because he truly felt he had done no wrong — was too much for me to emotionally process.

But like it or not, his death set the grieving-and-memorializing process in motion, and I needed to pack a suitcase and go "home." There was no time to process, just to act. Due to Skyler's limitations when it comes to traveling and sleeping anywhere other than his custom bed at home, Josh and I decided that Kendall would accompany me on the nearly five-hour drive to my childhood hometown of Marshall, Michigan. We planned to spend several days with my sister while helping my aunts and uncles with preparations for the burial and "celebration" of my father's life. By this point, Josh and I were very accustomed to a parenting "divide-and-conquer" lifestyle, so it was no big deal for me and Kendall to start the road trip first and wait on the guys. Josh and Skyler would plan to join us on the day of the funeral — traveling a torturous total of 10 hours round-trip by car to Jackson, Michigan, and then back home to Southern Indiana the same day.

I had been able to better process everything when the time came to pick Kendall up from school. I shared with her about my dad's passing and she told me she was sorry and asked if I was okay. I told her it had been an emotionally draining day, but that she and I would be going on a road trip to Michigan the following week. Although she didn't really know my dad, she was eager to be by my side to support her Aunt Beth and me.

The constraints of the COVID-19 pandemic caused some hiccups in the funeral planning, but a week following my dad's death, Kendall and I packed our bags, filled my white Ford Edge with gas, purchased our favorite driving snacks (Sour Patch Kids and Cheese Pringles for her, Peanut M&Ms and Baked Lays for me), and ventured down memory lane during our drive "up north." Quite unexpectedly, the mother-daughter road trip to his funeral would present the perfect opportunity to unpack those uncomfortable memories and address Kendall's curiosity about my childhood and resulting estrangement from my dad — the grandfather she never knew.

The Ride Home:
Conversations With My Daughter

I t only took about 30 minutes into our trip for Kendall to begin firing questions at me — about my dad and about my childhood, about the town we were about to visit and the family members we were going to be spending time with, many of whom she'd never met. It was clear that she had an expectation that I would fill her in on the first 18 years of my life. How else were we supposed to pass the time? It would turn out that sharing the numerous stories I had hidden away would be enlightening for her and both eye-opening and healing for me. The conversation that followed was one of the most important ones of my life.

Kendall had visited my hometown a handful of times over the years, but they were usually for brief weekends with a specific event monopolizing much of our time there. Despite the physical distance between my childhood home and my new life near the Indiana/Kentucky border, my sister and I prioritized such "family events" as often as possible. Our kids would be together to celebrate holidays and special occasions (birthdays, graduations, and stage performances) and develop a relationship with their cousins like we had with ours. However, as the kids aged and the travel constraints with Skyler became tougher to manage, Josh and I found it easier to divide and conquer, so Kendall began making the trips to Marshall alone with me, just like this one. I know she found entertainment in the candid interactions and banter between siblings — the dynamics between Beth and me, and also between her cousins Maddie and Will with herself — but I couldn't help but wonder if it also made her sad to know that she and Skyler would never have a brother/sister relationship like theirs. Skyler has never been able to communicate verbally and rarely interacts with Kendall at all.

Interrupting my straying thoughts, Kendall repeated a question she had just asked and that I left hanging: "It's pretty where you grew up, but it seems boring. What did kids do for fun?" I know what a chore it is to convince our kids that life could be enjoyable and entertaining before the invention of the internet, but I tried my best to paint an ideal picture of my unwired life in the '80s and '90s.

I grew up in the very small, very sheltered town of Marshall, Michigan, where it seemed every one of the town's approximately 7,000 residents knew your name and often your personal business. The main downtown is lined with historic old buildings that generally cover all the basics — locally owned diners, shops, pubs, a bakery, a hardware store, pharmacy, post office, hair salons and a few banks. All is within walking distance of the high school, middle school, library, and hospital with the famous Brooks Fountain serving as the town anchor. It is the classic Midwestern downtown. A slice of Americana. Sort of.

In addition to the historical buildings, the surrounding blocks of Main Street feature homes refurbished to their original 1800s glory. Visitors travel from all over the country to attend the Marshall Historic Home Tour, where they can parade through the antique structures to learn about the architecture and the history of the original owners. It's an idyllic town. If you don't dig up too many secrets.

Not only is the town picturesque in terms of the "curb appeal" of the homes and the shops, but there are low incidences of crime, and neighbors look out for one another, which to a teenager was both comforting and annoying when your parents knew what you were up to before you even had the chance to *act* on any mischievous ideas.

As a kid in the '80s and early '90s — before home computers, the Internet, cellular phones, streaming television providers, and social media were commonplace or even invented — it was an unspoken expectation that we would find non-criminal ways to entertain ourselves on weekends and summer breaks. The possibilities and potential risk for "actin' a fool" expanded after securing a driver's license on your 16th birthday.

A common pastime for teenagers in a town with absolutely nothing to do — at least back then — was to "cruise downtown," which consisted of a few blocks down Michigan Avenue and back, then up to McDonald's and the newly added Burger King. Rinse and repeat. Each car and truck cruising that path was packed full of kids and loud music pumping, as if it were a competition for whose bass speakers, jacked-up trucks, and loud engines could command the most attention. On hot summer nights, I could always find half my high school classmates downtown. If the streets were quiet on a weekend, there was a strong likelihood that our other form of self-directed entertainment — a party on someone's vacant property — was secretly happening. Those two activities sum up my high school years in a nutshell: cruising and land parties. Back then, I didn't assign any meaning or recognize the significance of those countless, carefree hours spent with friends outside my home, but I know now that those innocent, stress-free moments were my only means of escaping the trauma of my childhood. The "comfort" of home was where danger lurked, and "the big, bad world" was my safety net. All children of abuse and neglect under-stand this stark, ironic reality.

Kendall probably had no idea that asking me the question about "what kids did for fun" during my youth in Marshall would get me talking about things I'd never shared with her — silly stories and outlandish stories and eventually some painful stories too. I didn't talk about my childhood much — it was a topic and a set of memories I chose to avoid. But here, in this car on this breezy fall day while driving along I-65 and I-94, headed to a somber family reunion and a funeral for a man who I believed loved beer more than he loved me, there was so much to share with her.

I had plenty of friends who were "Townies," as we nicknamed them, based on them living in the heart of town, and I always wanted to be one, too. Townies were able to walk to and from school, which would've been amazing for me because then I wouldn't have had to always remember to carry a quarter for the pay phone so I could call my mom to ask her to pick me up after cheer or soccer practice. And Townies were in the heart of the action all the time — they were only mere steps away from all the city-planned events and activities, like the county fair, the July 4th BBQ, and the Christmas parade. Even though our house was located only three miles outside of town, the cornfields that flanked the front and back, as well as the constant complaints from friends who had to drop me off "all the way out there," garnered my older sister, Beth, and me the label of "country kids."

I kept taking time to glance at Kendall to see if I could "read" her as I shared these stories — to see what she thought of the stories about her mom and her aunt, her grandparents, and the town she was headed toward on this long drive across the flatlands of the Midwest, straight up the entire length of Indiana. She seemed amused. Aside from finding the act of cruising hilarious and the "land parties" an odd way to pass the time, Kendall did think the walkability between school and all the businesses and buildings would've been cool, so I'll take that as her validation that our means for surviving "the old days" didn't sound so bad. Indeed, it could have been worse. But it also could have been so much better.

Proceeding up the interstate, the car filled with laughter as Kendall teased about how terrible it must have been as a kid growing up in the '70s, '80s, and '90's having to watch only three channels of television (ABC, NBC, CBS) and listening to music on a cassette tape, whatever that was. I pleaded my case — that we had the best television and movies — and reminded her that MTV and other cable channels revolutionized home entertainment by 1990. This is one of many small moments that, when she revisits it in her mind, I hope will bring a smile to her face: When she thinks of time spent with me in the car. That has always been the location of our deepest conversations. When I was young, there was rarely any joking or fun in the car (or anywhere else). My sister and I were expected to be silent and not speak unless directed to do so, even if we had to pee or attempted to launch a complaint that we couldn't breathe because of the cigarette smoke my dad was blowing all around us. To this day, the smell of cigarette smoke makes me sick to my stomach and, to be honest, infuriates me that I frequently must walk through a gathering of smokers blowing their toxic cloud in my face to enter a business or restaurant.

Until that moment — until that road trip with my teenage daughter one week after her grandfather died — I hadn't really discussed much with Kendall when it came to the darker side of my childhood. I never felt there was an appropriate time or reason to bring it up and, considering she never really knew my dad, it didn't seem necessary. However, while discussing the highlights of my quaint hometown, I reminded Kendall that she actually met her grandfather once when she was three at the July 4th downtown BBQ, of which she had no recollection … and insisted I was mistaken. My sister had transformed Maddie and Will's wagon into an adorable red, white, and blue sailboat for Kendall and her cousins to ride in as participants in the bike/wagon parade. Shockingly, my dad made an appearance at Brooks Fountain (the end of the parade route) and briefly said hello to us and introduced himself to Kendall. But she was only three and probably pre-memory at this point. So, we would have to agree to disagree whether this event happened until we arrived at my sister's home to fact-check — where the mutual scrapbooking hobby I shared with Beth would come in handy. I was confident my sister had that rare moment preserved in a carefully crafted Creative Memories album.

"No, no … I've never met your dad," she said. The fact that Kendall has always called my mother "Nana" but instead uses the term "your dad" (rather than Grandpa, Papa, or any other affectionate term noting an actual relationship to *her* and not just me) when referencing my father is not lost on me. And it's sad.

There was, as it turns out, much to tell her about my dad — the good, the bad, and the ugly. So, with many hours to go, seated next to a captive and intrigued travel partner, I braced myself for an emotional but important drive down a very fissured and bumpy memory lane.

A Bumpy Road:
Learning Patience The Hard Way

Kendall and I continued chatting about me having grown up in the boonies and, honestly, I told her that it was perhaps a blessing in disguise to be hidden away from prying eyes as a "country kid" because of the very loud and very embarrassing language and abuse instigated daily by my dad.

"Is that why you hate it when people around you are yelling?" Kendall asked.

That was exactly it, and I told her so. The yelling was always filled with swearing and vulgar words to get his point across (or, I guess, to make us afraid of him). I learned every cuss word imaginable before the age of 7, which is why I never swore or allowed swearing around Kendall and Skyler. "Trust me," I told Kendall as we drove past miles and miles of cornfields, yellowed by fall, "I had to fight really hard some days to hold back my potty mouth, since it comes so naturally to me when I'm angry. But I did it because I never wanted my children to learn those obscene words from me."

"Well, you've sure given up the fight the past few years, haven't ya?"

"Zip it, Smartass," I bantered. And we both burst out laughing.

With nothing but time on our hands and a desire to be fully authentic with my daughter in this priceless moment of her rapt attention, I decided to tell her everything… And I did.

For my entire life, my dad was an alcoholic, clearly battling some significant internal demons. He refused to seek help or find the strength to overcome them, though I'd like to think he tried. Looking back at the way he behaved in public — not just at home — I find it shocking that he maintained his employment as a salesman and a delivery driver. The sheer number of uncomfortable confrontations I witnessed with family friends and members of the community due to his short temper and belligerent attitude, often a direct result of excessive drinking or being hung over, was outrageous. He was even arrested for driving under the influence of alcohol (DUI).

I'll never forget his arrest for drunk driving. In the wee hours of a weekday morning, primary school dreams consuming our deep sleep, Beth and I were startled awake and shuffled off in our footed pajamas to the neighbor - so my mom could rush to the county jail and bail him out. We did not have the extra money for bail. But she knew if she refused to bail him out and left him there overnight, he would miss work in the morning and might get fired from his job. And she knew that he would give her hell to pay if that happened. Of course, in that scenario, the outcome of losing his job would also conveniently be my mom's fault because he never took responsibility for any of his irresponsible actions and behaviors. My dad was gaslighting my mom long before any of us knew what gaslighting was.

As I was sharing these stories with Kendall, I could see lightbulbs going off in my head — so brightly, it was a miracle I could keep driving. I would utter details about my childhood in a matter-of-fact way, and I'd immediately feel it in my body — my heart and my gut and my head — and I'd suddenly see how the little girl I used to be had no choice but to become the adult (and the mother) I am now.

Half of what came out of my mouth during that road trip with Kendall felt like a confession or a "letting go" while I put the puzzle pieces together. "You know firsthand that I'm a worrier about everything, particularly when it comes to you and Skyler or things that are ultimately out of my control," I told my daughter. "Well, the thought of my father driving drunk and hitting or killing someone in my small town — someone I would probably know — was likely the reason I developed that trait. I carried that heavy concern and fear with me every day throughout childhood and adulthood, even after moving away, until he died. In the past few weeks, I haven't had to worry about him killing someone on the way home from the bar." Kendall responded in disbelief, "I can't even imagine having to worry about something as serious as that, Mom."

My mom — Kendall and Skyler's Nana — worked at the County Building for 33 years, and she knew (and knew them well) practically every lawyer, judge, and police officer in town. You'd think that being surrounded by the justice system would keep you safe, but it sometimes works out just the opposite. I think my mom was always afraid to call the police on my dad when he was abusive because it was a small town where everyone talked. But one horrible day, when she was literally backed into a corner and fearful for her safety and ours, my mom swallowed her pride and embarrassment and made that dreaded 911 call to ask for help. I was roughly age six and recall when two Michigan State Troopers — which is the irony of living barely outside the city limits and thus out of the jurisdiction of the local Marshall Police, who weren't permitted to respond — lights flashing and sirens blaring, squealed into our driveway, and rushed to the front door. As my mom tried to let them in, my dad blocked the door, forcing them to push the door in around him. He stumbled but didn't fall.

One of the officers addressed my mom by her first name — Judy — as he calmly gave her instructions. The humiliation on her face as she, my sister, and I were escorted outside — all while a hostile confrontation ensued with my dad — is pierced into my memory forever. She pleaded with the officers not to arrest my dad because, deep down, she knew it would only make matters worse, so she was advised to leave and drive around with us while my dad "cooled off." As the three of us drove away, tears streamed down all our faces. After driving just a mile down the road, the trooper who was following closely behind our car turned on his lights and pulled us over. That scared me to death, and I remember worrying that we were somehow in trouble now, too. As he walked up to her car window, I recognized him as the officer who called her by name back at our house. He said he just wanted to be certain we were all okay and asked if she needed any additional help, which she declined. He offered his sincerest apologies to all three of us and lowered his head as he walked back to his patrol car. It was that exact look of pity on the faces of every person who became closely involved in our family drama in the years to come that left me feeling perpetually embarrassed and wishing I had a "normal" family. It's all I wanted — a normal family.

I remember being petrified to go home. We didn't know what he was capable of, and we imagined the worst. This was my first memory of needing police escorts to safely exit our home to get away from my father. I'm sure the worrier in me, even back then, knew that the next day, everyone would act as if nothing ever happened — that was our loop. Violence and fear followed by denial and resolve. Loop de loop de loop.

I took a breath after recounting the details of that traumatic night and Kendall said she would've been humiliated, too, if neighbors or friends saw a police car at *our* house. Then she asked, "Did he mostly just yell and get mad at *Nana?*"

"No, Kendall. *None* of us escaped his verbal and mental abuse."

I glanced at her before returning my eyes to the windshield and I saw what I think was pain and sadness on her face. I'm not sure she'd ever really thought about me as a little girl. And I can almost guarantee she'd never thought about me as a child of abuse.

I was about 5 years old when I began to comprehend (and sadly retain) all the hurtful names my father called me: dumb ass, fat ass, smart ass, bitch. Every explosive confrontation he subjected us to — day after day — excluded none of us, until we were old enough to escape to a friend's house or drive away in the car I shared with my sister, Beth. We did "hard time" in that house. The words my father chose to spew in our direction were crude and foul — words that never should be hurled at another person, let alone his wife or little girls.

My dad was a small man — 140 pounds, 5 feet 7 inches tall. However, regardless of his physical size, he always loomed large. The angry boom of his voice and the piercing look of hatred on his face, both when he was drunk and sober, was a frightening sight to behold as a young child. Behind his back, my sister and I frequently referred to him as the dictator, Napoleon. No matter my age, when I heard "LAURIE!" shouted up from the basement or hollered from the backyard, I trembled as fear instantly set in. I always worried and wondered, "What did I do wrong or what ridiculous "chore" was he summoning me to do?" Perhaps I drank the last glass bottle of Pepsi without asking or made too much noise while playing and being a child. And maybe he was going to order me to turn the knob on the woodgrain console TV to change the channel because he didn't want to get up from the couch to do it himself. Those were the only two possibilities — I'd done something wrong or I was going to do something under duress — and neither ever resulted in a pleasant outcome.

The intimidation and vile speech were routine — we were subjected to them every single day. The only difference in the rotation between more subtle intimidation and outright verbal abuse was that one resulted when he was sober but hung-over, and the other occurred during drunken tirades. No one in our house was immune to his insults and abuse. He'd finish up berating my "dumb ass" then move on to let Beth or my mom know what worthless pieces of shit they were, too. Some of his favorites that often made the daily insult reel were, "You're a fat ass," "Stop being a dumb ass," "You're useless," "Stop looking at me with that smartass look on your face," and "You better hope you don't turn out like your bitch mother."

While recounting these traumas to my daughter, she shrieked, "Holy *crap*, Mom!" I'm so sorry he said all those things. What a *jerk*! Thank you for not calling me names like that!"

I was a bit shocked by her response — not for its truth (my dad *was*, in fact, a jerk), but because it validated that my conscious effort to build up her self-confidence rather than default to tearing it down (as I'd experienced) had not gone unnoticed. I was a good mom who had grown up with an awful father. Bit by bit, I realized that I had broken the cycle of abuse.

It was a profound moment on an Indiana highway. Wanting my daughter to know how much I loved and respected her, and wanting to break some of the tension, I told her, "I appreciate everything about you, Kendall. You truly are a remarkable person who is capable of anything … and you are the farthest thing from a dumb ass." That made her chuckle and the sound of her laughter made me smile. I forged forward, telling her more of my story so that she could understand who we were headed to Michigan to memorialize and bury.

I told her that my dad's verbal abuse wasn't just reserved for the school year. In fact, the two-week vacation he took from work every summer proved to be one of the most dreaded times of the year for me and Beth. Our dad insisted that we get out of bed super early to get started on the various chores he had assigned, like picking up rocks in the front yard (that had been innocently tossed there by cars driving by) or weeding *his* damn garden until he decided the job was complete.

I shot a loving glance toward my daughter, who was listening intently and eating Pringles at this point, her shoes discarded in the footwell of the passenger seat as she casually wiped the crumbs from her favorite hoodie onto the floor of my SUV. "Honestly, Kendall, you should consider yourself lucky that I've never asked you to do yard work," I said to her and then winked. "Shoot, you complain about your one chore of feeding the cats."

I said it kindly, with zero guilt-trip vibes, but still knowing that comparing my childhood to hers might help her expand her worldview at this critical teenage moment — as she was growing up and heading into a world that might not be as safe, loving, and idyllic as what she'd known all these years in the carefully crafted family that Josh and I had created for her and her brother, Skyler. That statement about the cats garnered no comment, other than a deep sigh and an accompanying eye roll.

I forged ahead with my story, telling her that it was no surprise that her Nana purposely chose to work during my dad's vacation time. It was wise and self-protective for my mom to avoid all that one-on-one time with my dad, but it left me and Beth on the front lines to deal with him by ourselves. Without our mom there as a buffer, Beth and I had no one to help plead our case to just lie around and enjoy a lazy summer break, like our friends were doing. You better believe we called my mom's office at least twice every hour to whine and complain about the unfairness of it all, which annoyed and irritated her.

Focused more on the "not sleeping in" part of my story than the chores, Kendall interjected, "How early was 'super early?'"

Knowing my child never wakes before noon unless forced to do so, I said, "Let's just say it was hours earlier than you're used to getting up, and you would've hated it."

She nodded and observed, "Well at least now I know why Skyler being up at 6:00 a.m. every day doesn't bother you. You're used to it." *Oh, kid. You have no idea how bothered I am.*

I redirected our conversation back to summer chores and told Kendall that the only "benefit" to come from tending the garden was selling the fruits of our labor (well, *vegetables* in our case) at our highway roadside card table or in the bar.

It was quite the production. Every spring, my dad planted a huge garden in the backyard and told us how fun it was going to be to grow our own produce. Months later, when the weeds were outgrowing the sweet corn, cantaloupe, green beans, radishes, strawberries, onions, potatoes, squash, and tomatoes, you could bet one of the Sullivan girls would be loudly summoned outdoors to pull weeds or gather the harvest completely against our will. After we had bushel baskets full of produce, it somehow became our job to sell the shit. We were bribed with promises that we could keep all the proceeds to use as "spending money at the county fair," so as any young kid excited about making money would do, we agreed. That is until around 5th or 6th grade when those bribes no longer worked.

For what seemed like hours, we sat at the card table along Old US 27 in the scorching hot sun, complaining, whining, and praying one passerby would stop and buy everything so we would be allowed to close up shop. Just when we thought we couldn't take it another minute, my dad would shock the hell out of us and agree to let us call it quits. Before declaring victory and running off to play, Rocky made us load all the unsold products back into the bushel baskets and told us we were going on a field trip — an invitation we were never permitted to decline (at that powerless age, at least). We should have known he'd use this moment as a perfect excuse and business opportunity to head to the bar at the most opportune time of the day — when all his drinking buddies were nicely sauced.

My dad was born a salesman. From his childhood paper route to his adult career selling lunch meat to grocery stores, I learned everything I know about the fine art of customer interaction and closing a sale from him. We pulled up to the bar, carried in the goods, and my future career in sales was born. The first person who asked why I had such a sad face became a sucker (I mean, Customer Number One). I easily launched into my story about being stuck in the scorching heat all day, and no one would stop, so we had all this produce — which took us an entire morning to pick from the garden — left for sale. Eyelash bat. My dad stood back and watched. His fellow bar patrons told my dad how horrible it was to make such adorable little girls suffer like that and, within minutes, the entire lot was sold, including the bushel basket it was stored in! It was like an auction; the purchase offer increased with every pout and sad face I made. I guess to reward himself for some fantastic parenting, my dad kept us in the bar for several more hours as he consumed countless beers and kept us sugared up with Faygo pop and our favorite drink, a Shirley Temple. This scenario played out multiple times, summer after summer until Beth and I no longer wanted to go to the bar – together or separate.

Kendall stopped me mid-sentence and inquired, "A what? What in the heck is a Shirley Temple?"

"Oh Kendall, they are so good," I said. "It's a mixture of 7-Up or Sprite with maraschino cherry juice blended in. When served in a fancy bar glass, Aunt Beth and I thought we were such fancy 6- and 7-year-olds, sipping on those red-colored drinks."

We three —Beth, my dad, and I — were a package deal at the Riverside when my dad was on vacation and therefore "on duty" as a father. He took us with him to the bar, so Beth and I could keep each other entertained and so he could avoid any parenting responsibilities. It didn't work if he took just me or just Beth; if only one of us was there, we would whine nonstop and repeatedly ask when we were going home. I think my dad's bar friends also enjoyed us hanging around and essentially assisted my dad in babysitting us by giving us quarters to play Ms. Pac-Man, pinball, and the jukebox. They also occasionally let us "play" pool when no one else was busy with the cue sticks. His routine Saturday visits to the bar presented a different scenario – one where Beth or I had to be 'selected' to tag along with him.

Like clockwork around noon, my dad would holler out "Who wants to go to the hardware store?" to which Beth and I would compete as to who responded first. We both knew that "hardware store" was code for the bar, and the lucky kid who got to ride shotgun would not only get out of cleaning the house with my mom but was in for a full day of sugary treats and hand numbing arcade playing – and all weekend bragging about being the favorite!

However, winning the 'hardware store game' quickly lost its allure roughly around age 11. If we didn't have weekend plans with friends taking us away from home, Beth and I would beg our mom to tell him we couldn't go. Knowing we'd be complaining and making his 'me time' miserable, he finally quit asking and we all enjoyed a full Saturday apart.

Because this was my childhood, talking about it felt natural even though I know it's not "normal" to take your kids to a bar. Interjecting again as I shared the details, Kendall appeared dumbfounded by this part of my childhood: "You and Aunt Beth were playing in a *bar* when you were in first and second grade?"

Completely understanding her shock, I responded, "Actually, my dad started taking us there even younger than that!"

You would think that a bit of "bar bonding time" with our dad would periodically end well or create overall "happy" memories, but that was never the case. Tired of washing glasses behind the bar (yes, the bartenders allowed us extremely underaged minors to assist behind the bar!), bored playing arcade games, and wired from all the sugary drinks, one of us would often sneak away to the avocado-green rotary phone hanging on the wall inside the greasy bar kitchen to call our mom, unknowingly starting World War III. I distinctly recall her response being the same each time I called. She would always angrily say "Where are you?!" as if she didn't know and then followed up with, "Put your dad on the phone." Now, at that moment, I had two options: I could either tell my dad that I called Mom and she wanted to speak to him, or I could lie and say Mom called the bar looking for us and would like to talk to him. I always chose the latter to lessen the blow I'd receive if he knew I called and tattled about the fact that we had been at the bar *all* day.

I would hear him speak into the phone receiver for roughly the length of two heated sentences before slamming it down and declaring to me and everyone in the bar that he was going to "finish his beer, *then* we would head home." In actuality, and to send a message to my mom that no one tells Rocky Sullivan what to do, he would order one more beer after sitting back down, and we would not leave until *that* beer was gone. And when we did, we went home via motor vehicle with a drunk driver.

It is truly unbelievable — as I look back on it now — the number of times strangers, friends, and family members, including my mother, allowed us to ride unbelted in the front seat of that powder blue 1979 Lincoln Continental with our completely shit-faced dad … knowing the consequences could result in us being killed or killing someone else in a drunk-driving accident. What was "normal" for us was not just immoral, but illegal. But nobody seemed to care.

"Wow, Mom, that's pretty awful."

Yeah. It is. I can't remember whether I said that to her, or if I just sighed and surrendered to the feelings of having my teenage daughter express compassion for my former childhood self. It was all surreal and profound.

Sharing these untold stories with my daughter, no matter how uncomfortable or emotional it makes me, has helped provide so much insight into my own parenting choices and decisions for Skyler and Kendall. I am the parent I am today because of the child I was then. This clarity — this understanding that I'd been on a difficult but *purposeful* journey to become the parent I need to be for my kids — was an outcome of my dad's passing that I didn't anticipate, but has become so beneficial to my healing, growth, and perspective.

I recognize now that the millions of times my dad lost his shit for no rhyme or reason had as much to do with his insecurities as it did his inability to relax and not overreact. He was the poster child for sweating the small stuff. We are not born patient because wailing and panicking is hard-wired into us to help us survive as infants. But by the time we are adults — especially by the time we are parents — we need to exhibit patience. Patience is a character trait we learn through life experiences. But I didn't learn it from my dad.

Like most children, I relied heavily on my parents to demonstrate and teach me the benefit of being respectful and calm when interacting with others. Unfortunately, I inherited Rocky's impatience and ease of irritation when things don't go as planned or as quickly as I believe they should. Now don't get me wrong, I don't unleash rage-filled rants filled with hurtful names on anyone within earshot, aside from the occasional curse words screamed from behind the wheel when cut off or tailgated by an inconsiderate driver. But raising my voice or displaying obvious frustration through body language are actions I always promised myself I would never inflict upon my children. However, I must be honest and admit that there have been many instances throughout my own parenting journey where I've launched into unnecessary shouting and arguing or overreacted to a situation — responses mostly born from instinct without taking a breath and thinking before mimicking my dad's behavior. I'm human, and I'm still learning and growing. I used to view each instance of losing my cool with my kids as a parenting failure and feared that I was creating another generation of hotheads. But, as a continual work in progress myself, I recognize that this lesson on self-control and slowing down to enjoy each moment is one that Skyler, Kendall, and I have learned together.

My children, by default, are inherently impatient people and are quite intolerant of things that don't come easily to them on the first try, but Skyler's inability to verbally communicate adds an entirely unique set of challenges within our mother/son dynamic. I can't begin to imagine what life is like for him and the level of frustration he experiences daily when trying to accomplish a task independently or have his basic needs met with no voice. I feel as though I'm playing an endless game of charades with him, trying to understand what he wants or what he's trying to tell me. If Skyler appears uncomfortable or in pain, I must literally probe his body from head to toe in search of probable causes and rely heavily on my mother's intuition. It's overwhelming and heart wrenching to know your child is hurting and you are unable to determine the cause and resolve it. Annoyed with my inability to read his mind, Skyler often reacts in the only way he knows will gain my undivided attention — aggressive behaviors. He hits; he pulls my hair; he bangs his palms and fists on walls, counters and doors; and he will throw every free-standing object he passes to the floor as he continuously paces a loop around the kitchen and living room. Many of these instances of unrelenting agitation have led to significant discoveries about his health — most notably, his long overdue diagnosis of Crohn's disease, so I have a considerable amount of empathy for how badly he must feel for things to become so dire that physical outbursts are necessary. When he was younger and smaller, I could simply ignore the smacks and assaults on my ever-thinning hair while continuing my mission of solving the mystery ailment and fixing the problem. So, one might think that after almost 20 years of dealing with repeated physical attacks, my tolerance and ability to compartmentalize these moments from the happy times would be almost second nature. But you would be wrong.

As I said, I'm a continual work in progress, and my temperament and body are far less forgiving as I age. During a particular moment of weakness after months of incessant hitting, as tears streamed down my face, I recall screaming at Skyler, "Stop hitting me! Don't you understand that I'm desperately trying to help you? It's not okay to treat your mom like this. No one outside of this house is going to put up with your abuse as communication!"

Anytime I lose self-restraint and spew anger and negativity, it's as if Rocky's voice has infiltrated my own. I become disappointed in myself, despite how far I've come with maintaining my composure, specifically when encountering all the uncertainty that follows an autism diagnosis. The look of shock and sadness on Skyler's face immediately makes me regret my tone and harsh words. Of course, I feel like a complete asshole for getting mad at Skyler for communicating his discomfort and frustrations in the only manner he knows how. Behavior *is* communication. I immediately apologize for raising my voice and for my choice of words, which is something my dad never did or considered doing, and I explain in a much calmer tone that I promise to do better at regulating my tone and response the next time I'm feeling frustrated. I also look Skyler directly in the eyes and tell him, "It's not your fault" (a line I stole from Robin Williams's character Sean Maguire in the Oscar-winning motion picture *Good Will Hunting*), which surprisingly makes him smile and giggle, signaling to me that I'm forgiven. And if I'm being honest, I curse my parents for teaching me no coping methods other than yelling or throwing a tantrum during times of struggle.

Although I've worked hard at managing my triggers and quickness to anger from my interactions with Skyler, parenting Kendall is vastly different, in large part because she has no problem expressing herself and using her large vocabulary to loudly challenge or argue her point of view. Two of Kendall's difficult traits I wish she hadn't inherited from me are her constant pursuit of perfection and stubbornness, which she prefers to describe as "confident in her opinion." ("I'm not stubborn. I'm just confident in my opinion!") But stubborn as she is, she's also quick to quit anything she can't do perfectly on the first or second try. It has always frustrated and confused me how quickly and angrily she would throw in the towel on an activity, if she didn't achieve instant success. For example, we made countless efforts throughout her youth to teach her to ride a two-wheel bike. From the start, her expectation was to dump those training wheels and instantly ride off into the sunset on her first try, but when her first few attempts resulted in falling to the ground, she bolted back into the house and swore off ever trying again. Her convictions have held strong to this very day — so much so that a mountain bike did not make the packing list for college.

Just as Skyler's nonverbal aggression can sometimes trigger a lapse in my composure, Kendall and I know how to push each other's buttons. And because we are both headstrong and competitive, neither of us is ever willing to concede defeat or let the other have the last word. Her indifference and repeated "Who cares?" comments at the onset of a discussion used to make me go nuclear, widely opening the door for my irritation and temper to stomp on through. Instead of letting cooler heads prevail, thus creating a teachable moment about rational thinking and respecting a different point of view, every conversation resulted in a heated argument. Regardless of the topic, because the volume of my voice rose to match or exceed hers, Kendall always inferred that I was mad at her and wandered off to her room, leaving the matter unresolved. Dumbfounded at how I let the situation go so far into proverbial left field — and disappointed that I seemed to be failing miserably at breaking the cycle of invoking fear into my children by ranting like a lunatic — I applied the same thought process about regulating my tone and demeanor with Kendall as I had begun doing with Skyler. I'm happy to say that we had remarkably strong results. Instead of letting our discussions escalate to an argument, feeling like I needed to match her tone or go toe-to-toe with her until she realized I was right, I instead maintained my composure, steadied my voice, and listened more than I spoke. I learned from my therapist the importance of leading with the following question before Kendall shares what's on her mind: "Do you want me to provide suggestions and feedback, or do you prefer that I just listen?" It's mind-blowing how that one introductory question has changed the entire dynamic of our relationship and has allowed both of us to walk away with confidence about how to move forward. It's a beneficial life lesson that we learned together and one that will undoubtedly serve us both well in the long run.

While I'd love to declare that I learned the importance of exhibiting patience exclusively from viewing the effects of my short temper through my children's eyes, it wasn't that "cut and dried." It has been my husband Josh's jovial demeanor and ability to relax or pause, rarely appearing rattled or angry, that also made me want to match his energy and, frankly, be a better mother with a more loving and consistent tone. While I've made many valuable adjustments to my temperament, watching the kids gravitate toward Josh during times of uncertainty or an emotionally charged situation continually inspires and motivates me. From the moment he entered our lives 13 years ago, when Kendall was 6 years old and Skyler was 8 years old (at the perfect time, I always say), Josh has been the rational, calming presence Skyler, Kendall, and I needed. Josh is just an amazing human who loves large and makes anyone feel secure, seen, and heard. He is exactly who I needed in my life after having first been married to my children's biological father, an emotionally void, uninvolved partner and parent.

I have learned that it is sometimes in my best interest and Skyler's that I step aside and let Josh take the lead, particularly when Skyler is feeling the anxiety that comes with navigating new experiences — like riding a horse and venturing into the community or the familiarity of a seasoned routine that he's most comfortable doing with Josh, like walking laps around the mall for exercise or frequenting Skyler's favorite restaurant for lunch every Saturday afternoon. Watching their daily interactions and the way Skyler responds with smiles and laughter to Josh's sing-songy tone of voice as he cuts Skyler's hair or carefully straight-razors the five o'clock shadow from Skyler's adult face makes my heart melt. *That's* what a good father looks like.

Similarly, there are often moments with Kendall when fatherly advice is the preference. So, part of my growth in becoming a more patient parent has been embracing the moments I'm needed for guidance or support and respectfully taking a back seat when Josh is summoned over me. God placed Josh in our family not just to be a role model for my children who adore him, but to help guide me in processing my childhood dysfunction and repurposing it to develop meaningful, healthy relationships. He's the patient, understanding dad to our kids I wish I'd had, and I'm grateful Skyler and Kendall have him.

As I evolve and continue to learn how to maintain a calmer, less frantic way to support and encourage Skyler and Kendall throughout their lives,

I have found that the fraction of impatience I let marinate in the background still serves a valuable purpose. There are times when I must push and challenge therapists, medical providers, and state agencies to take immediate action on Skyler's behalf instead of letting them sit idly by while a "wait-and-see" approach is unwarranted or even dangerous. The uncharted road of adulting with nonverbal autism requires a guardian, mother, and caregiver who is a fierce advocate, intolerant of people who underestimate or disregard my son. So, although I've grown leaps and bounds with my ability to be patient, I intend to hang on to the critical little piece of me that expects some things to be handled with a sense of urgency, particularly where Skyler's future health and wellbeing is concerned. I will always be the little girl who's willing to pick up the bar's backroom telephone to call in a favor, call for help, or call in a complaint. I have finally learned that it's okay to speak up after a lifetime of being fearful to do so.

3-Point Turn:
Seeking Validation, Strength and Confidence

Kendall seemed to be hanging on to my every word, absorbing the details of my childhood and gaining a bit more insight into me as more than "just her mother." Capitalizing on the pause in conversation, I turned up the radio volume a bit, purposely set on the Sirius XM Totally '80s channel, which Kendall humored me by not complaining about. One song after another, my favorite songs filled the airwaves: "Rhythm of the Night" by El Debarge followed by Lionel Richie's "All Night Long," and I proudly belted out every word, much to Kendall's clear dismay. I always find it fascinating that not only can I remember song lyrics from 40 years ago, but that the moment I hear them, I'm transported back to my age of the song's release and can recall very vividly a memory tied to it. These two specific songs triggered a slideshow of joyful, summer memories made with my sister and our neighbor, Kim.

"Aunt Beth and I were tired of only having each other to play with, so the best thing that ever happened to us was when Kim moved in during our middle school years," I recalled to my daughter.

Kendall had met Kim, who served as a bridesmaid when Josh and I wed, but Kendall apparently hadn't realized we'd known each other for that many years.

"I thought you said the summers were just as awful as any other time in your house," Kendall said, lilting her tone just a tiny bit to make the observation into a question.

"Well, not during the day when all our parents were at work," I corrected. "Outside of that two-week vacation my dad took, we found lots of ways to have fun during the three months of summer break!"

Again, what piqued Kendall's immediate attention was the lengthy summer break from school. *Three full months?!*

"It was awesome, Sis. In Michigan, we ended school in early June and didn't start up again until after Labor Day."

Clearly disgusted at the year-round schedule our school system observes and that Kendall has been subjected to much of her school-girl life, she responded, "That's totally unfair."

I started calling Kendall "Sis" when she was little. Her favorite books — which I read aloud to her until she was old enough to read them herself — came from my old and very large collection of Berenstain Bears books, by Jan and Stan Berenstain. In those beloved books were two characters — the Berenstain bear cubs — named Brother Bear and Sister Bear. Given Kendall's love for the book series, she naturally earned the nickname "Sister," which eventually got shortened to "Sis" … and it just stuck.

Laughing at Kendall's comment about long summers being "totally unfair," I launched into a slew of stories about Kim and the way she, Beth, and I spent our summers. Each day during those middle-school summers, we three girls would rotate who got to select the song we'd use, then we'd spend hours choreographing dance routines and digging into each other's closets for costume accessories. Despite having to alternate garages to use as studios and stages — and the poor sound quality of the cassette tapes played on the small speakers of the boombox — it was quite the production! Sometimes we would have neighboring kids or friends over to watch, but we mostly just enjoyed the laughter and freedom to enjoy the summer without being yelled at.

Kendall laughed at the details of my story and, in her most judgy, teenager tone said, "Sounds lovely, Mom, but you lost me at cassette tapes and boombox."

I retorted again with, "Never mind that part, Smartass," only teasing with the name-calling (despite its appropriateness for the storytelling of my childhood, where such terms were never ones of playfulness and endearment). *My goodness*, I thought — how the world has changed. My children had never heard such words used with anger or derision. And it was a small miracle that I'd learned to play around and "needle" my kids in a harmless, loving way — no longer afraid of the words that had once made the hairs stand up on my body or made me want to run away somewhere safe.

Safety is exactly what I had delivered to my children, every single day of their lives. And love. And respect. Their childhood — if I was doing my job right — was nothing like mine.

But we were connected by our histories and our interests. Kendall is a lot like her Aunt Beth when it comes to her love of books. Much like Kendall, my sister Beth utilized stories and fictional settings to transport her into a calmer environment when she was feeling stressed. For me, music and dancing were my chosen escape route to a safer, happier existence. The imagination is a powerful panacea for what ails us (and a defense against those who hurt us).

"Did you and Aunt Beth always dance together? The old videos you *made* me watch always showed both of you," Kendall asked as the car chewed up mile after mile of that long drive to Michigan.

"Excuse me? I never *made* you watch. I highly encouraged you to join me as I strolled down memory lane. You gotta admit, Kendall — we were pretty awesome dancers back then."

"Uh huh," she replied with yet another eye roll. Just because I was driving didn't mean I didn't catch those expressions. I smiled back.

Music and dance were an important part of my childhood, formally and informally. My mom was a dancer as a child, (until her stepmother abruptly cancelled her dance lessons with no explanation before my mom started high school) so I think introducing her daughters to dance classes brought back fond memories and meant a lot to her. Beth started at age four, and I would enroll the following year when I turned four – since that was the required age. I was so jealous of Beth's black leotard, black tights, and eventually her recital costume that I could barely stand it! But, finally, after what seemed like an eternity watching her skip in and out of Miss Bobbi's Dance Studio, seemingly living her best life, it was finally *my* turn to follow in her literal footsteps. I joined the "tiny tots" combination tap and jazz class and fell in love the minute I strolled through the door. Slipping my tiny feet into those shiny new black tap shoes — with the smiley-face elastics to hold them closed and the exciting clippety-clop sound they made as I walked onto the giant dance floor — I instantly felt at home. Because I was always unable to sit still, I thrived in a place where kids were encouraged to move freely and enjoy themselves while also learning valuable skills — like following a beat and counting.

"Mom, you are still always on the move, so this makes a lot of sense," Kendall interjected.

Miss Bobbi would teach us one or two new eight-count combinations a week to add to our routines, which I practiced every chance I got without my mom having to hound me to do so. I would've danced down the grocery store aisles to entertain people, if she hadn't quietly suggested that perhaps watching me do the Charleston or shuffle ball change in the produce aisle may be a bit of a distraction to the customers who just wanted to grab their bananas and go.

My mom reminded me that the annual dance recital, which took place in late June, would be the perfect place to showcase my skills. Let me just tell you, from my first recital to my very last — my senior year of high school — dance-recital weekend was my favorite weekend of the year. The costumes, music, and stage designs were carefully crafted around a central theme, and the entire two-hour production was coordinated flawlessly from start to finish. I felt like a star.

"Does this help you understand why I used to go kinda nuts with excitement during your recital weekends, Kendall?"

"Yes, Yes it does, Mom."

I felt like a bubbly little kid as I told my daughter all about it. I found myself trying to convince her that attending a Bobbi's Dance Studio recital in the auditorium of Marshall Middle School was the hottest ticket in town "back in my day." Performing under those bright lights and hearing the loud applause rewarding my efforts always made me feel special and truly seen, which is something I so desperately wanted and needed at that point in my life.

"I'm guessing your dad didn't come to your recitals or ever watch you dance?"

In the early years, I shuffled onto the stage, eager to spot my mom in the audience and always hopeful my dad would be sitting next to her. I pictured him cheering me on and afterward rewarding my efforts with flowers and praise like all the other dance dads did for their children. None of that happened for me. Instead, I quickly learned that his attendance presented yet another opportunity for him to publicly humiliate me. I can count on one hand the number of recitals he showed up to, and he acted like a drunken fool at each one. Conveniently, he left before the show was over because he didn't like watching other people's kids dance and likely wouldn't have been capable of standing still for any photos.

To be fair, there was one recital I know he attended because he actually *danced* in it! The dance dads seemed a little envious that the dance moms had a recital number, so, for a few years—and delightful surprise to the audience—the dads performed a recital number, too. The year prior to my dad joining, the dad's 50s number to "Rock Around the Clock" connected to our jazz routine, which included a moment when the kids posed with their fathers. Rocky hadn't been part of that dance, so Beth and I posed with other people's dads. I have absolutely no idea how my mom convinced him to do it— maybe he felt guilty that we had a stand-in dad prior—but the following year my dad was willing to be in the 'King Tut' number. Our optimism was unprecedented. And clearly misplaced. The perfectly punctual 7:00 p.m. start of the recital meant that we were actively engaged in either performing or changing costumes, so we didn't know until intermission that Rocky hadn't arrived at the middle school auditorium yet. Mild panic set in. *We* knew where he'd been. What we didn't know was what kind of condition he'd be in when he showed up.

When he stumbled in shortly before their number took the stage, the three of us knew he was drunk. But he wasn't belligerent and seemed 'with it' enough to get through the performance. In the end, he managed to do most of the dance correctly, but I distinctly remember and can still feel the embarrassment of having the only dad in the group who was hammered. All we'd wanted was to fit in and have a "normal" family, but we should have known better. It's not like anyone said anything directly to us, but it was likely a moment that solidified for our dance family the understanding that Rocky was indeed an alcoholic. And they probably understood why it was usually just the three of us without him at every dance event. My dad's turn as a dancer was a one-and-done experience, and recital weekends returned to our "normal." Mom always left his ticket on the kitchen counter—next to his wallet and keys, so he couldn't miss it—before we left the house on recital mornings. Many times, post-show, we'd return home to find the ticket sitting in the same spot where it was left; my dad, his wallet and keys were the only things missing. We pondered the same thought year after year: *Maybe he'll show up to watch us and maybe he won't.*

Rocky was neither reliable nor supportive when it came to any of my sports teams and events. Similar to his disinterest in my years of devotion to dance, I don't recall my dad's attendance at a single one of my soccer games, nor did he ever show up for a football game to watch me cheer throughout my four years of high school. Again, he preferred not watching other people's kids. His absence was his only predictable character trait. The only public participation he gave to my cheerleading is when he showed up, stumbling drunk, to the football stadium just in time to escort me, alongside my mom, as I was recognized as a senior cheerleader during the homecoming game my final year of high school. Having a good story and "proud parent moment" to discuss while sitting at the bar the next day is what motivated his once-in-a-blue-moon presence at my social activities. While those sports were enjoyable to me, his inability to give two shits about my true passion for dancing or ever getting to know me as a person imprinted a deep-rooted disappointment and accompanying self-doubt within me. I feel it still today and could sense myself grappling with it while talking to Kendall about what it was like to be a kid back then — what it was like to be *his* kid. "Geez, he really didn't care if he hurt your feelings, did he?"

"No, Kendall. His response the few times I asked why he chose not to be present was that recitals were too noisy and too long. Frankly, I don't think he felt comfortable, nor was he capable of being sober in public with his family. I think he meant that recitals were 'too long' to be sober and 'too noisy' for a hangover."

I paused and ruminated on it all for a moment, and Kendall let me stay lost in the reverie, saying nothing.

Then I took a cleansing breath and said, "Let's get back to happier memories from the dance studio, shall we?"

When Beth and I were around ages 6 and 7, my mom dusted off her own dance shoes and decided to join Miss Bobbi's mothers' class. Initially, her practice night was on Wednesdays, so because our lessons were on Fridays at that time, her participation meant that we would be at the studio now two nights a week. This gave my dad a convenient excuse (not that he ever needed or provided one) to drive straight from work to the bar on Wednesdays because my mom wouldn't have his "goddamn dinner on the table" if he were to come home. If you can't eat, you might as well drink.

After several years of just tap and jazz, I was eager to try some new styles. I believe I was in second grade when I added ballet classes and in third grade when I added baton lessons, to my weekly tap and jazz classes. I was so excited every Friday because instead of walking to our babysitter's house from Hughes Elementary School, I got to ride the Dial-a-Ride van, which was Marshall's public transportation, for the short commute to the studio. My mom's one rule was that our grades and homework didn't slip, so once we proved that we could handle dance and school without issue, she let me and Beth continue adding lessons, which also meant spending more nights at the studio each week. It was a welcome escape from home.

Throughout middle school and high school, I was in multiple groups — lyrical, jazz, tap, and clogging; a jazz duet with Beth; and two solos. To say we began practically living at the dance studio was an understatement.

The four walls, one comprised of floor to ceiling mirrors, of that tiny studio was our sanctuary. My mom really enjoyed being there, too. It was honestly one of the only times I recall her having an outlet to be social and engage in joy and laughter. I'm sure she preferred to let the conversations about costumes, competition details, and organizing fundraisers with her fellow dance mom friends temporarily give her peace. Beth and I weren't the only ones who "ran away from home" to be at the dance studio.

It was fun to talk to Kendall about the happy parts of my childhood "dance life" and to connect with her over this shared passion and experience. I told her, "Just like my time spent at your studio, Kendall, Nana enjoyed every single moment. From gluing rhinestones on swimsuits to create last-minute costumes when ours were on backorder to screaming the loudest and crying the most when we were on stage, it was her happy place as much as it was ours."

Age 11 was the moment everything regarding dance ramped up and got even more exciting for me. Miss Bobbi only allowed a small number of solos, duets, and the occasional trio to be entered into competitions and performed in the recital, so when she invited me and Beth to compete with a new jazz duet, we were thrilled. At the same time, Miss Bobbi was putting together new competitive jazz and clogging middle-school teams, which Beth and I were also invited to be part of. Unlike Kendall's more modern experiences, we didn't have to audition to be on the competition team. Miss Bobbi hand-selected the dancers with the strongest skills and most potential when she formed the teams. My duet with Beth and our group routines were winning so often that we became studio "favorites," and most importantly, my mom and Miss Bobbi could see how much I loved competing. So, at age 13, I was given a clogging solo and jazz solo and added those to the competition circuit. Dancing was becoming the predominant feature of my life.

Fast-forward to today, with a teenage daughter who had spent 11 years in dance training and performance, and I know how expensive dancing can be, especially when you add all the travel and extra costs associated with competing. My parents often struggled to have any money left over after the bills were paid (including my dad's bar tab), so I don't know how they were able to afford it. But my mom never flinched, at least in our presence, and always made it happen with a smile on her face. It's heart-wrenching to think about it now, as an adult — how much my mom probably sacrificed to make sure Beth and I were able to keep doing the sport we loved.

Truly though, one of my favorite parts of competing, whether it was a regional or national competition, was that it was almost always just the three of us — me, my mom, and my sister, Beth. There was only one competition my dad attended, and it was a big one that we earned entry into from our regional wins — Rising Star National finals — which iron-ically was held in downtown Louisville, Kentucky, where I would one day attend many competitions with my own daughter. My mom, ever the optimist, wanted to make it into a family vacation (because we rarely took one), so we drove from Michigan to Pigeon Forge, Tennessee, for a few days of Dollywood theme-parking, where my dad decided to finally act like a doting parent … to a kid named Darren we'd met in line at a ride. While generally stingy and grumbling whenever we'd asked for snacks, Rocky had no problem doling out cash and attention for this random kid who ended up spending the entire afternoon with us, riding all the coasters seated next to my dad. Considering my dad never willingly spent quality time with me aside from making me spend a full day at the bar with him, it really stung to watch him buddy up to a stranger the same age as me — this kid who seemed to be navigating the park alone. My dad always told us he never wanted girls, but this chosen demonstration of neglect was next-level cruel.

Other fond memories of this trip include my dad being in a bar across the street during our group jazz performance to Frank Sinatra's 'New York, New York,' which ended up earning us the most prestigious award of "Top Group" for the entire competition. We never took another family vacation after that, and he never attended another dance competition.

I sort of wish I could have given up on him at that point — that I could have found a way to ensure he never crushed my dreams or hurt me like that again. But I guess I was still desperate for validation or some demonstration of love and support from my dad because I held out hope for that supportive "dance dad," year after year. Time and again, the moment we arrived home from a competition, I'd run beaming with excitement into the house — first-place trophies, ribbons, and medals in hand — to tell him of my success. Without fail, he continually crushed my spirit and instead of sharing how proud of me he was, he chose to complain. "You mean to tell me that I spent all that money for competition entry fees, hotels, costumes, and dance lessons and all you got was another goddamn, cheap, plastic trophy?"

Thank goodness Kendall never knew what that felt like. When she came home from a competition, her bonus dad, Josh, greeted her at the door and showered her with excitement, congratulations, and a beaming smile. Once he even taped a sign to our garage door which said, "You crushed it! I'm so proud of you Sis," because he knew we would be getting home super late and, in case he was asleep, he didn't want her going to bed without knowing that. I won the jackpot when I found Josh, and so did my kids.

Ever the believer in "second chances," there's a part of me that always thought maybe my dad would get his act together in time to "get it right" for his grandkids. I've heard stories from friends and colleagues who have shared that parents who really dropped the ball in parenting them eventually stepped up to become good grandparents. "Better late than never," I suppose. But Rocky didn't bother to step up for his grandkids either. His neglect of and disinterest in me and Beth extended to his lack of relationship with Kendall and Skyler, and with Beth's kids, Maddie and William. But as adults, Beth and I have watched my dad favor someone else's kids -over his own grandchildren. It was a repeat of him choosing Darren! He never once watched Kendall dance, and my sister had to beg him to travel less than a mile from the bar to the middle school to watch Maddie's recitals … and he still didn't go. Ironically (and painfully) though, a bartender's daughter took dance lessons from the same studio as my niece, and one year, when the recital was being repeated on two different nights,

Rocky went to see the other girl — the bartender's daughter — dance but didn't go to see his own granddaughter.

Rocky had, time and again, been performative in his "fatherly" activities for other adults and children, to the exclusion of his own. Over many years, he quite freely 'loaned' money to strangers due to one sob story or another, rarely getting a dime of it back. Meanwhile, Beth and I have been solely responsible for managing our financial needs (including college) since we left home at 18. Sadly, none of his grandchildren ever received a gift or greeting card from him either. So, yeah, you could say I've felt a little slighted all my life.

For all the ways in which my own biological family came up short, there were others who became "bonus" family. One of the most important people in my young life was Miss Bobbi, our dance teacher, who became a significant member of our family. Having one son and no daughters, Miss Bobbi took great pride in us, her "studio daughters," and went above and beyond to make us feel special inside and outside of the studio. Miss Bobbi was an incredibly talented seamstress. I remember the excitement in her eyes months before our high school's homecoming dance and prom each year, when several of us would ask her to make our custom, one-of-a-kind, formal dresses for the dance. We always invited her to attend the pre-event photo sessions with our dates, and seeing her eyes tear up when she saw each of us wearing her finished masterpieces was so touching. She loved us and we loved her, unconditionally. Beyond the dresses, my connection with Miss Bobbi seemed to deepen once she started to truly see the negative impact my dad, the drunk, was having on my self-worth. There was no hiding our dark reality from people who were truly close and paying attention. Instead of defaulting to only positive feedback and compliments to encourage me and boost my confidence, she challenged me with some of the hardest choreography and placed me in a position to teach and inspire the younger students. She knew I needed some extra "parenting," some opportunities to grow, and a safe place to try new things and even fail. My love of performing and self-confidence increased with every year, thanks to the devotion of Miss Bobbi.

She truly was one of a kind.

When I reflect back on those thirteen enjoyable years enthralled in all things dance, I hoped that one day I might have a daughter who chose to follow in her Nana's and my footsteps by participating in dance. Aside from the glitter, applause, and flowers, dancing enhances many important skills – coordination, confidence, and character.

The moment I learned I was pregnant with a little girl, I began envisioning her in tutus and tiny tap shoes, taking center stage. I honestly couldn't wait to take my turn as the annoying "dance mom" at recitals and competitions — that all-too-excited mom who insisted on taking too many pictures, cheered too loudly, and was easily brought to tears at how beautiful and talented her daughter was on stage. Although I desperately wanted the opportunity to share my love of dance with my daughter, I never pushed the idea and waited for Kendall to ask me if she could join the local dance studio. Thankfully, I didn't have to wait long because she asked to go to "tap school" with her pre-school buddies at three years old.

I'm sure, like most moms, I recognized early that my child had talent. I mean with her pedigree, it's not much of a surprise. Ha! Seriously though, she demonstrated quick memorization of the choreography while accurately and effortlessly mimicking the teacher's movements. Kendall was very comfortable on stage, the crowds and bright lights not fazing her a bit. She was so happy when performing, and I couldn't have been prouder.

Around age 10, Kendall seemed to be getting bored with recreational dance and wanted more of a challenge. Having watched the competition teams perform at the studio recitals, she approached me and asked if she could audition. After weighing the pros and cons and gaining her commitment that the increased practice schedule wouldn't negatively impact her grades, I gave her the green light. She made the Youth Pom dance team and ironically started her competitive dance journey at age 11 … just like me.

Kendall continued dancing competitively in pom, hip hop, and jazz for five years, and throughout that time, her team won several regional and national awards and earned two bids to The Dance Summit in Disney

World. The conclusion of competition season in early 2020 brought along a very unexpected turn of events — the COVID 19 pandemic, which ended face-to-face physical contact for a painfully long period of time. The studio dance recital typically held in May was canceled, and the year abruptly ended as we hunkered down into a forced quarantine in our homes. Earlier in the season, Kendall had contemplated quitting dance because her heart wasn't invested anymore, but admittedly, I didn't take her mentions of quitting that seriously. However, a few weeks before the 2021 season was to start, she told me that she was not going to dance anymore. My initial, selfish response was filled with anger, disappointment, and sadness as many unsolicited opinions and comparisons to my childhood ran through my head. Rather than seek to understand why she was making this choice or praising her for the confidence and courage to do so, I instead reacted just as my dad would have, speaking without listening.

With an elevated tone, I peppered her with my thoughts. "Do you realize how lucky you are to be cheered on and supported by so many family members — specifically Josh, who proudly wears his 'dance dad' t-shirt at every competition? I would've loved to have had my dad in my fan club."

I was also annoyed and sad about the loss *I* would endure from her decision. Being that this was Kendall's only extracurricular activity and that we had never found anything for Skyler to be directly involved in, her decision to leave the dance team subsequently eliminated my only outlet for developing relationships and connections to a group of women and moms whose commonalities, for a change, had nothing to do with autism. I also felt robbed of the opportunity to spend Kendall's last few years of high school bonding over a shared interest and celebrating my daughter's wonderful talent, which was leaps and bounds beyond mine. Simply put, I loved being a dance mom, and Kendall's decision to quit dancing took that away from me. I was beyond devastated but had unknowingly and unintentionally made it all about me. My epic parenting failure at handling this situation may have sent the wrong message and weakened her confidence, which was the exact opposite of what I'd meant to do.

I will never forget the day that Kendall told me she was done with dance — the day I handled that very mature and thoughtful decision on her part with very visceral and uncontrolled emotion on mine. The look on Kendall's face in response to my frustration provided an instant flashback to myself at her age. While slightly different, I felt myself reacting to her quitting similarly to my dad questioning his "sacrifice" that had only been paid back in "cheap plastic" trophies. What I'd wanted back then, as a younger dancer and a troubled man's little girl, was validation for a job well-done, and what I wanted now was validation for a parenting job well-done. This situation provided yet another moment throughout my motherhood journey where I had the chance to reflect on my own childhood experiences, change my natural inclinations, and in this case, redirect the focus off myself and back to Kendall, where it belonged. What she was seeking from me was validation that I would still be proud of her and love her regardless of whether I agreed with the decision she made. I needed to be a parent who recognized that, honored that, and modeled that … because that's what my child deserved. I loved the daughter, not the dancer. And I needed to make that distinction in my mind.

Parenting can surely be humbling — especially when roles are reversed and your kids are the ones providing life lessons and teachable moments. I swiftly apologized to Kendall for reacting selfishly and assured her that I fully supported and understood her choice to move on from the dance team. Even more important, I told her that I wouldn't trade a single memory throughout those 11 years accompanying her to every dance practice and performance. Truly, the greatest gifts to come from that time spent with Kendall was watching her develop self-confidence, poise, and the courage to spread her wings, while I learned to listen, trust, and let my little girl soar.

Looking at her in the passenger seat of my car, truly comfortable in her own skin and seemingly without a care in the world, I knew that

Kendall was my little girl, growing into a remarkable young woman. As if on cue, the next song on the radio was entirely fitting.

"Kendall, you're probably going to roll your eyes, but this is *another* song Beth and I danced to for our jazz duet," I laughed as I reached over to turn up Paula Abdul's 'Forever Your Girl.' "The music gods are with us today!"

Time was passing quickly due to the nonstop conversation in the car. Road trips have a way of passing in a blink or dragging on forever. In the car, it's like reality is suspended and we live "in between." This is true for all road trips, but there is something especially difficult and surreal about traveling to a funeral. On the way to a funeral, it's easy to talk about anything — to avoid the sadness and stark reality that awaits you at your destination. And while Kendall and I had spent hours talking about my dad and my sister, my mom and the younger me, it didn't seem that any of it had prepared us for what we were about to do. We were about an hour away from the Great Lakes State and, for the first time since we pulled out of the driveway, the car was silent. I glanced over to the passenger seat and asked Kendall if she was okay. She paused, an expression of sadness on her face, before responding that she felt bad my dad didn't support me and that he didn't at least pretend to care. Yet again, I'm thankful her own experiences with competitive dance (and life) didn't mirror mine. Understandably, more questions followed.

"I know he said lots of horrible things to you, but did he ever hit you guys?" she asked.

Buckle Up:

Releasing Our Secrets

I took a deep breath and hesitated for a brief second. This felt like a watershed moment.

My sister and I often brought up childhood memories when it was just the two of us chatting, but I hadn't really felt it necessary to share some of the scariest events of my childhood with my daughter. Until now. I guess maybe I felt that *this* moment — on the highway on the way to my daughter's grandfather's funeral — was the right time to tell her the ugly truth.

I took another breath. "Well, Kendall, I'd tell you to buckle up for this, but since you already are buckled in ... here's Story #1" ... and I proceeded to answer her question honestly and with detail.

My dad's drink of choice was beer and there was always plenty of it at our house. And if he ran out, it was a great excuse for him to leave for the night, presumably to buy another case at the party store that was a couple miles from our house and conveniently located next to his favorite bar. I can kind of measure time by the brands of beer he drank: Cans of Pabst Blue Ribbon lined our fridge in my elementary years and Bud Light bottles from middle school on. And I'd imagine that because he smoked for over 40 years — usually Winstons in the red package — all those beers tasted flavorless and watered-down anyway. But I doubt he drank it for its taste as much as having a beer in his hand (and alcohol in his veins) was his identity. Maybe he thought it defined him: a hard-working, blue collar sonofabitch who was the king of his castle.

I don't know why, but whenever hard alcohol like whiskey entered the picture, he was like a man possessed. Like the Hulk, my dad's inner beast

— Raging Rocky — became violent the minute he stumbled through the door. Those nights were the scariest of my life.

A lot of times, he would just be emotionally hurtful and destructive of our property, hurling insults and objects at us before retiring to the basement and passing out on the couch. But Kendall had just asked me if he was ever physically abusive. So, I did my best to paint a picture for her, as I'll do here for you, as well.

I was 13. We had a finished basement in our little ranch house, and that's where most of our TV viewing took place — on the three broadcast channels we had back then. My mom and I were watching a movie, and Beth was babysitting at a neighbor's home for the night.

Our peaceful Saturday evening was interrupted by the familiar sounds of unsteady footsteps stumbling through the doorway and keys slamming on the kitchen counter. Without uttering a word, my mom and I exchanged eye rolls as we mentally braced ourselves for the typical insults and yelling that was surely headed our way. My dad bulldozed his way down the stairs and after he turned the corner, my mom and I could tell by the devilish look in his glassy eyes that he drank whiskey — not just beer — that night.

"Where's my fucking *dinner*? Why are there goddamn dirty *dishes* in the sink? How many times have I *told* you or those fucking *girls* of yours about leaving dishes in the sink?" my dad roared.

I'm still unsure how she managed it, but my mom timed her exit from the TV area as he lurched forward, and she hightailed it upstairs for a much easier escape route out of the house should she need it. Staying in the basement might have been a grave mistake. Shockingly, my dad had the balance and stamina to pursue her up the stairs, all while hollering, "Don't you walk away from me, you fucking *bitch*!" — because walking away from Rocky's attention-seeking tirade only fueled his anger even more. As my mom attempted her getaway, she screamed, "ROCKY STOP! Just leave me alone!"

I stayed, terrified and alone, in the basement. I initially stood at the base of the stairs, listening, and eventually worked up the courage and curiosity to quietly climb the stairs.

After what seemed like five minutes of screaming and cursing between them, along with my mom's pleas for my dad to "get away from her," his tantrum progressed into heaving every random item from our kitchen countertop, along with each dirty dish and piece of silverware in the sink, directly toward my mother's head. It was like a tornado in the kitchen.

I was scared shitless but remained silently crouched at the top of the basement stairs, inches away from where he stood at the sink — but too far away from where I knew my mom was standing to be of much help. I didn't know what to do.

After the clatter of silverware fell to the linoleum, I heard my mom rush down the hallway and attempt to barricade herself in their bedroom. At that moment, I was unsure of what to do but knew I had to do *something*. I wondered: *"Do I creep back downstairs and call 911 from the basement phone on his desk? Do I barrel past him and somehow try to guard my mom?"*

Before I could make up my mind, I heard a loud commotion and what sounded like my mom gasping and saying "Let … Go … Of … Me," only it came out as a strained whisper. She sounded like she was choking. Pushing aside my own fear, allowing rage to take over, I sprinted up the stairs, through our tiny kitchen and down the hall to find my dad had pinned my mom against the wall just outside their bedroom. His hands were tightly clasped around her throat. I thought he was going to kill her right there.

In sheer panic and desperation to save my mom, I ran back to the kitchen, grabbed the butcher knife, and charged back toward them. Through clenched teeth and with a confidence I never knew existed in me said, "Let her go." He ignored me, refusing to release his grip. My mom's face and neck turned from a deep red tint to blue. So, I moved closer and repeated myself, louder this time, shrieking like our lives depended on it (because they did): "I SAID LET HER GO!"

He turned his head and his rage-filled, bloodshot eyes glared back at me before he finally released his grip enough for my mom to escape. Through coughing and tears, my mom's only focus seemed to be on me. She yelled, her voice sounding hoarse, "Laurie, put the knife down," and almost appeared mad at me for getting involved. I followed her orders and put the knife away. In that moment, I was only focused on my mom and not on my dad. I don't even remember where he was standing or what he was doing as we walked bravely away, shaking and in tears.

Later, my mom would explain that she was fearful of the situation escalating to the point of no return — of her dying in front of me — with my future being ruined and with me and Beth motherless and with a father headed to prison. I had always imagined that what got her to walk out that night was her own survival instinct, but I think it was her maternal instinct — she wanted to save her children (and, of course, herself). Suddenly, I was sure she understood that being Rocky's daughters was awful and dangerous for me and Beth — that she wasn't the only victim caught in his control.

It had been over three decades since that fateful night, so I was able to talk about it with Kendall while keeping my composure behind the wheel. But it was all so new and shocking to her. She fumbled for the right words: "What did you and Nana do after that? How in the heck could you ever go back home?"

I recall my mom trying to regain her composure in the car before driving us a few blocks away to where Beth was babysitting. We filled her in on what had just happened and waited there until the homeowners returned from their date night. It was beyond awkward for Beth to explain why her mother and sister were on their couch when the husband and wife walked through the door, but more neighbors were aware of Rocky's behavior than we cared to admit. Perhaps it was because she didn't witness the attack on our mom firsthand or maybe she had just become immune to his antics by this point, but Beth seemed unfazed by the violence. We eventually made it back home and found my dad passed out on the basement couch.

Per our usual routine, the next morning, everything was "fine," and it's likely that my mom took me and Beth to church just like any other Sunday morning. We also went to school on Monday with fake smiles plastered across our faces like nothing out-of-the-ordinary happened over the weekend.

I looked at Kendall sardonically and said, "If you weren't sure what true resilience looked like, I would say this is a pretty damn good example!"

While I've carried this story with me through life and have talked about it with my sister, my husband, and my therapist, it wasn't really until after sharing it with my daughter that I contemplated how it's shaped me as a person and eventually a parent. We were never *directed* to bury, deny, and remain silent about frightening moments like these, acting as if they never happened, but that behavior was *modeled* for us by how quickly my mom dismissed the events and moved on. Even now, she refuses to discuss any stories from our childhood that involve my dad's violent nature. She refuses to validate the trauma of what we experienced and survived.

As the child of an alcoholic and overall severe family dysfunction, I never felt comfortable confiding in anyone but instead turned a lot of that trauma into intrinsic motivation to work my ass off at school, at the dance studio, in sports, and anywhere else I could channel it outside of that damn house. I could have gotten lost in the pain (as my father did after his own traumatic childhood), becoming burdened by the trauma so much that it could have negatively altered the trajectory of my teen years, my adulthood, my career — my entire future. But instead, I pushed through and now actually have some appreciation for the chaos. It was perfect preparation for the resilience this motherhood journey would require.

Lest I stop there, I continued with Story #2, telling Kendall about how my dad's behaviors failed to improve as Beth and I aged and as my mom stayed — year after year — in an abusive marriage.

There was another equally disturbing event five years after the choking incident that also involved my dad drinking whiskey. It was during one of my visits home from college, and all hell broke loose. Again.

Although I'd freed myself from my dad's bullshit and gotten the hell out of that house following high school graduation (something I'd hoped and intended to do for as long as I could remember), the separation wasn't entirely permanent. During Christmas break from freshman year of college, I had no other choice but to return home. Don't get me wrong — I wanted to be there for the holidays with my mom, but there was no way to completely avoid my dad during those few weeks between semesters.

By this point, my sister, Beth, had moved to Colorado to attend college and was not coming home that year for the holidays, so I was left to fend for myself. On this night, Mom was at work. She had taken a second job as a cashier at Felpausch — our main grocery-store in Marshall at the time — to help save money for Beth's upcoming wedding. So, there I was, back at my childhood home during a holiday break from college, with my mom away at work and my dad, as usual, was at The Riverside Bar. The house was quiet and peaceful. I was alone.

It was around 9:30 p.m., and I was curling my hair, preparing to head out with some friends to one of those "land parties" I told you about earlier, when our home phone rang. The voice on the other line was my dad's close friend and drinking buddy, Bill. He asked me the strangest question. "Do you have any guns in your house?"

Openly perplexed, I responded, "Um, that's a weird question, but no. I think we may have a BB gun in the garage. Why?"

I was not prepared for Bill's response.

"It's just that your dad has been spouting off at the bar all night about killing your mom, and he says he plans to shoot her, so I need to make sure before I bring him home that he doesn't have access to a gun."

I squealed, "What!?! Don't bring him here! He's obviously been drinking whiskey and is out of his mind!"

I was freaking out because, with my mom being gone, that meant he would surely make me — the only other person in the house he despised as much or more than her — his target. I didn't want to die. Or be abused or attacked in any other way. Less than 10 minutes later, several cars pulled into our driveway, driven by equally intoxicated men. My dad stumbled inside, held up by three of his enablers, with that devilish look in his eyes that I knew so well.

"Where the fuck do you think you're goin', dressed like that?" Rocky yelled.

His friends "tried" to quiet him, but no one can stop his tirades once he gets started. I ignored him, which pissed him off more.

"You aren't leaving this house until you give me money. If you're gonna use my electricity while you're here, you need to pay for it!"

Just as I was making my pleas to pay him later, my best friend, Alex, came to pick me up for the party. Having been my friend since grade school, he knew about my dad's alcoholism, but I could see that even he seemed concerned by the volume of my dad's voice when he walked in — Alex had never witnessed anything like this.

I was advised by the drunkards in my kitchen to warn my mom not to come home, so Alex and I left the house and immediately made a quick pit stop at "The Pausch," as we called it, to fill her in on the situation. She was surprised to see us but then laughed off my advice to stay away from our house. Per usual, I felt like I was the only sane person in my family who took these situations with Rocky seriously. I remember wondering: *"How does she not remember the choking incident or countless objects hurled at her face? More importantly, how does she not care about her own safety or mine?"*

As astounded now, from hearing this story, as I was from experiencing it firsthand back then, Kendall asked me, "So, what did Nana do then, since she didn't seem worried?"

My mom went home after her shift to find my dad passed out cold, no longer a threat for at least that night. As for me, Alex and his mom insisted that I stay the night at their house, which took zero convincing, and — just like every incident before — we would all carry on as if the chaos of the last 24 hours never happened. My father had openly plotted to murder my mother, and he wasn't held accountable. More importantly, we weren't afforded any measures of future safety either. Hell, we weren't even afforded the chance to process the trauma or speak about it in a way that might be cathartic and healing.

My daughter was shocked. "OMG Mom! I mean, these stories are seriously awful! How did you live like that for so long?"

Sometimes I'm not sure how I managed to deal with it, either. But I know now that it has shaped me in more good ways than bad. I learned how *not* to behave and to appreciate the family I created. I learned to treat myself, my spouse, and my children the exact opposite way my dad treated us. Perhaps, all along, what kept me going was the belief that I could and would break the cycle.

Given all that I experienced and survived as a child — and considering the challenges adult life has thrown at me, like my difficult first marriage and the trials and tribulations of raising a son with nonverbal autism — I have spent a lot of time in recent years thinking about virtues like patience and character traits like resilience. Much like patience, resilience isn't something we're born with; we learn it or inherit it. And what happens to us when we are young is vital to what kind of resilience we do or do not develop. Indeed, our early lives shape us.

Before having my own children, I'm not sure I would've used the word "resilient" to describe myself. While living through a childhood steeped in dysfunction, I viewed my responses and reactions to troubling situations more as a means of survival than strength. However, now that I'm a mother and a very vocal autism advocate, my perspective on strength and resilience has changed.

Whether it be from family, close friends, or virtual acquaintances, I frequently hear phrases like, "You're the strongest person I know. Kendall and Skyler are fortunate to have you." And "I don't know how you do it. I'm not strong enough to handle all that you do."

Initially, those compliments made me uncomfortable because I often felt anything but sturdy or confident when it came to parenting. After all, my parents didn't really equip me with the necessary tools or a roadmap to emulate raising confident, happy children. Couple that with a parenting path like mine (with children who have very different talents, capabilities, personalities, and medical challenges, and one who requires 24/7 care) — which looks considerably different from the "norm" — and it's a wonder how I don't break at the first sign of a challenge. However, being Skyler's and Kendall's mother has provided me the opportunity to embrace and utilize the countless skills I acquired, like resilience, because of my dad's alcoholism. I get to repurpose my past and use it to redefine the role of parent, as I see it. My past has empowered my present (and our future). And I happen to think that I was somehow chosen to parent these two very special kids. I was ready for this. I was, truly, made for this.

Just because some of my parenting skills and instincts come naturally doesn't mean it's all a walk in the park. I rarely view my parenting journey as seamless or easy. There have been many moments during motherhood when I've felt like a complete failure and wanted to throw in the towel. It's wrongfully assumed that the moment our newborn is placed in our arms, we automatically know exactly what to do — as if women are born with this innate ability to instinctively decipher every cry, fix every issue, and develop an instant and inseparable bond with our children. Unfortunately, that has never been my experience with Skyler.

Throughout his life, Skyler has been thrown significant curveballs — seizures, nonverbal autism, dyspraxia, anxiety, and Crohn's disease ... and none of those diagnoses came without a lengthy fight to get them, understand them, and address them. Medical professionals and experts refused to listen and trust in my mother's intuition when I pleaded with them that his refusal to make eye contact, his failure to respond to his name, or his inability to utter even a handful of words at age 3 was not because he was a boy and that boys often develop communication slower than girls. Or when attempts were made to convince me that Skyler didn't need a colonoscopy because his 4-5 straight days of constipation weekly for most of his life was not indicative of a more serious problem, but instead was commonplace with people on the autism spectrum and could be easily resolved with daily doses of Miralax.

Despite his various medical challenges, Skyler was born with limitless determination, courage, and adaptability along with the willingness to try anything at least once. Watching him joyfully tackle new therapy programs, such as horse riding, or experiment with new communication methods, like Spelling to Communicate (S2C), makes me beam with pride and in awe of his tenacity. No matter his level of discomfort or uncertainty and regardless of how long it may take him to succeed, he never quits trying. The effort and strength he exhibits every day is inspirational and serves as a constant reminder to me that I, too, have overcome hard things.

It was during those moments of challenging medical opinions and my refusal to give up hope or underestimate Skyler's growth, abilities, and competence that the resilient little girl within me was awakened. Until that time, I had never imagined that the mental toughness I developed from my childhood would become a requirement for motherhood, but God always knew, as this was an essential part of His plan. As I'm reminded daily, He prepares us with what we need, not always what we want. That mental toughness I earned as a child has served quite a valuable purpose in my quest to protect, nurture, and advocate for my own children. Where my own parents fell short, I hope to excel.

Aside from deciphering the mysteries and challenges of a nonverbal child, there have been many events in adulthood that have required me to move beyond my fears and vulnerabilities and, without much hesitation, gather the strength to do what was best for me and my children. Making the decision to divorce my first husband after a 10-year marriage and venture out on my own as a single mother was frightening, but more important to me was modeling for Skyler and Kendall the benefits of courage and a refusal to settle for a life of unhappiness (like my mother did). It's one thing to tell myself that I'm going to break the cycle of dysfunction I endured as a child; it's another thing altogether to actually do it.

Divorce is never easy, particularly when you're going through it raising children, one of whom has profound special needs. However, the choice to end that marriage was one of the best decisions I've ever made because it led me to Josh. Finding the courage to love again and be vulnerable — to marry again and to share my children with someone they could feel safe and comfortable around — makes me extremely proud of myself. I finally got it right — not just for me but for them. Surviving a childhood and first marriage where I felt alone and unworthy of being loved left me with a lot of emotional brick walls that were difficult to infiltrate. But this time, Josh was the resilient and patient one and, in the process, helped teach me the importance of nurturing our marriage during challenging circumstances instead of neglecting it. I had become so accustomed to managing *everything* in our household that relinquishing control to "allow" Josh — who wanted to contribute equally as a parent, caregiver, and spouse — was a foreign concept. I learned quickly that the energy of surrender accomplishes much more than the energy of control.

We make a great team, particularly when we're tested with Skyler's health issues, and I recognize how blessed I am to have found such an incredible husband who supports, encourages, and truly loves our often-crazy, unpredictable life. I'm the best version of myself with Josh by my side. This time around, 10 years of marriage is just the beginning. I know that Skyler and I have learned a considerable amount about overcoming challenges from each other and being chosen as his mother has taught me to appreciate and apply my own childhood lessons on flexibility, adaptability, and internal strength — resilience — that were perfectly placed within my past.

Cruising:

A Tour Through My Past

"Wow. I'm so sorry, Mom," Kendall said in utter disbelief when I finished telling her about the night that Alex and I left my raging father to warn my mother that he intended to kill her. "I can understand why you never talk about your dad. You must've really hated him your whole life, huh?"

I had to think for a minute about that statement before responding. This is exactly why my reaction to my father's death surprised me. For many years, I absolutely hated him to my core. I hated him for all the suffering he caused and for the way in which he robbed me of a carefree, safe, loving, supportive childhood. However, one day in my late 30s, post-divorce, I had an epiphany. I wrote my dad a letter — one that I never actually sent — and outlined all the ways he had hurt me and essentially ruined my childhood. I ended the letter by choosing to forgive him for not being the parent I needed him to be.

A few months after tucking that letter safely away in my bedroom nightstand, I decided to tackle my feelings head on by paying my dad a surprise visit, hoping to find the strength to forgive him in person, as I was able to do in writing. I had zero expectations for the outcome. This was something I needed to do for my well-being and mental health. My stomach was in knots the entire drive to Marshall, fearing the disastrous outcome of confronting my dad — in his preferred home, The Riverside Bar, nonetheless. I don't think it fully registered when he saw me enter the smoky bar and walk toward him. I saddled up on the empty stool next to him and he uttered, "What are you doing here?" in complete disbelief. I told him there were some things I needed to get off my chest and that I wanted him to just hear me out.

As I began reciting the memorized contents of my letter, he sat emotionless, continually sipping his beer until I was finished. Now, I predicted he would likely disagree with my recollection of many events throughout my childhood and protest with his own version of things, but what I hadn't prepared for was his complete denial that any of it even happened. My dad's only response to me that day was, "Laurie, it wasn't that bad." No attempts to gaslight me. No acknowledgment of the trauma he inflicted on his family. And certainly no apologies – not even a halfhearted one. Regardless of his refusal to take accountability for any of his 'parenting' choices and how they impacted my life, I got what I came for: closure in the only way I would ever get it — one-sided.

Choosing forgiveness was more for my sake than for his, as is always the case when it comes to hatred and forgiveness. In forgiving him, I was finally able to release the heavily weighted burden I'd been carrying for far too long. Holding tightly to that hatred for Rocky overshadowed the hard work I'd put in to fill my life and my children's lives with positivity and encouragement. I no longer wanted to harbor resentment for the memories from my past or continue to let his negative voice overpower my own.

"Not anymore, Kendall. No, I don't hate him," I proudly declared. "I released the hatred for my dad long before he passed away and felt pity for him when I learned that he left this world an unchanged, lonely man … full of anger and bitterness. He lost the game of life. How could I not feel sad about that?"

We were nearing the various highway exits of my hometown, and I asked Kendall if she'd like to cruise past my old childhood home. Of course, she obliged and was eager to have the helpful illustration that the little "tour" would provide for the stories I'd shared thus far. Seeing where those stories took place might help them further resonate with her.

As we approached the backdrop for many of my nightmares, I slowed the car and felt a wave of anxiety engulf me. Sadly, it no longer resembled the house I grew up in. In February 2001, my dad, (who remained in the home alone after my mom finally divorced him in 1996) in a drunken stupor, knocked over a shadeless lamp setting the carpet in Beth's former bedroom ablaze. The house, along with many of my adolescent belongings, burned completely to the ground. That was a lovely phone call to receive at 2:00 a.m. from my sister, telling me that all my stored keepsakes were now piles of water-soaked ash and soot. The house we were looking at now was rebuilt by my dad, in a similar shape and design as my childhood home, but once he moved out a few years later, its lack of curb appeal and run-down exterior made it almost unrecognizable to me. Nevertheless, I could still paint a clear picture for Kendall of what it looked like — growing up "in the country" on 17-Mile Road.

I pointed to the far-left front window, I said, "Kendall, that room at the end of the house was my bedroom, decorated in peach and mint green. I'm sure I don't even need to tell you that it was the most organized, tidy space in our house."

Knowing my fascination with color-coding and organizing every square inch of our home — from the closets and drawers to the pantry and the garage — Kendall was not a bit surprised to learn that I've been a compulsive organizer my entire life.

"So that's why you get annoyed when people don't put things away exactly as they found them," she teased.

"Exactly! Being hyper-sensitive about my things as a kid really came in handy when your Aunt Beth took something of mine without asking then tried to put it back, assuming I wouldn't notice. She could never fool me! Trust me, Kendall," I explained, "her sneaky 'borrowing' caused many sister fights when we were teenagers."

The virtual "picture this" tour from the front seat of my car continued with my parent's room, which was located directly behind mine at the end of the hallway. (The location of the hallway choking incident, I reminded her).

"For as long as I can remember, my parents had a huge waterbed — which I refused to lay on because it gave me motion sickness — that took up nearly all the floor space. The middle front window was Aunt

Beth's dusty rose bedroom, the large front window, which was a bay window when we lived there, was our living room. Our one small, shared bathroom was across from Beth's bedroom with the galley-style, eat-in kitchen positioned behind the living room. As you know, also from the choking incident, we had a finished basement and large backyard with an in-ground pool, added to our home when I was in the 3rd grade, and of course my dad's cherished garden. Our home was a nicely decorated, quaintly sized residence for a family of four, which Nana took great pride in keeping clean and orderly, as long as my dad wasn't around to disrupt things."

Now that Kendall had the lay of the land, we proceeded northward on 17-Mile Road, toward what I like to call Rocky's weekly "bar crawl." About a half mile down the road from our house was an establishment called The Moonraker.

"Kendall, this bar was often my dad's last-ditch attempt to get one more beer into his already-sauced body before coming home from his night of drinking elsewhere. The crazy thing is, despite how close it was to our house, he constantly risked getting pulled over even in that extremely short distance. Every Marshall police officer knew the car he drove — I mean, it was the only powder-blue Lincoln in town and was an easy mark. I never spent much time in that bar because it was built after I was old enough to refuse his invitations to tag along. I never sold vegetables to the drunks at *that* bar."

Kendall and I traveled another mile north and arrived at The Moose Lodge, where — of course — my dad was a proud member. The Moose Lodge had a bar.

"Although Aunt Beth and I weren't at this bar as often as our next stop on the tour, we did spend a fair amount of our childhood here. Sometimes, we were there for a purpose, representing our dance studio as performers in every Christmas event, but mostly we were forced to tag along with Rocky and gain some questionable new insights, like the fine art of gambling in the form of pull-tabs." For those who aren't familiar, pull-tabs are multi-layered paper tickets with symbols behind the tabs.

If the winning combination is "pulled," the ticket can be exchanged for a cash prize. Every time we got whiny and begged to go home, our dad would buy a few pull-tabs and let us keep the winnings, essentially paying us to shut up. Ironically, much like driving while intoxicated with us in the car, this was yet another illegal activity we were unknowingly roped into participating in — considering minors under 18 aren't allowed to play pull-tabs.

"For me, the worst part of visiting this establishment was the giant moose head coming through the back wall that scared the shit out of me. My dad always claimed—and swore on his life it was the truth—that the moose ran directly into the wall and got his head stuck, and that's how it ended up there."

"What an awful lie to say to a little kid who was already afraid of it!"

This kid gets me. And she cares. I smiled weakly and said, "I know, right? Trust me Kendall, that damn thing is still there, which is why we are just doing a drive-by tour instead of stopping in for a visual because, to this day, it still gives me nightmares!"

Aside from playing with the pull-tabs and annoying the patrons with our repeated attempts to "play" more than "Chopsticks" on the piano, Beth and I used to kill time at the Moose Lodge bar by sipping Cherry Cokes through tiny stirring straws and trying to invent new ways to entertain ourselves. It was rare to find other kids our age (or any age, really) in the bars. We considered ourselves lucky when we'd walk into a bar like the Moose on a Saturday afternoon and find a few potential playmates running around.

Venturing another few short minutes up the road, Kendall and I arrived at my dad's preferred destination and, one might argue, his second home — The Riverside Bar. Ironically, the apartment constructed 20-30 yards from the back door of The Riverside literally became my dad's home for roughly the last decade of his life. Having visited my dad in his Riverside apartment once, a few months prior, Kendall was much more familiar with this location (and my disdain for it).

Traditionally, my infrequent trips back to Marshall began with an unannounced stop at The Riverside, where I would attempt to engage Rocky in a very brief chat, much resembling the 1993 movie *Groundhog Day*: same scene, different year. I would enter the gloomy, smoke-filled and stale-beer-scented air of the dive bar (a bar that considered itself a classy pub!) and I always found myself cringing with disbelief that he preferred this daily routine and depressing establishment over spending time with his family or being outside or doing literally anything else. Every weekend (and, once he retired, every weekday), from after breakfast (though sometimes he ate breakfast there, too) and reading his morning paper to well past sunset, there he would be — occupying the same corner barstool, outfitted in ill-fitting jeans and an oversized sweatshirt, which purposefully hid his malnourished frame. A new, ice-cold Bud Light bottle was placed in front of him, perfectly timed as if it were an unstated expectation between my dad and the bartender that a fresh beer must be waiting in reserve before he polished off the last drop of the current one held tightly in his arthritic hand. In between sips of beer, he further "calmed his nerves," as he used to say, by chain-smoking Marlboro Red cigarettes. Keep in mind, this was well after smoking inside bars and restaurants in Michigan (and most everywhere in the U.S.) had been outlawed. Yet there he was, smoking away like he owned the place and like he was above the law.

I did my best to explain to Kendall what it was like to have those "bar visits" with my dad these past several years. "The one thing I never shared with you, Kendall, is how awkward it was when I tried to engage my dad in conversation during an impromptu visit. Never one for demonstrating emotions outside of irritation and anger, he would skillfully acknowledge my entrance through the doors with a straight-faced glance and slight nod in my direction, perhaps miming disbelief that I willingly showed up there. I always felt so damn uncomfortable, and it was clear he did too — which was ironic since I spent much of my childhood in that bar. Too late to turn around and run, I would slide into the adjacent stool, plaster a fake smile on my face, and spend the time it took him to finish his next beer telling him what was new with you and Skyler, not that he ever demonstrated interest in actually hearing about it. As usual, I would be reintroduced to the same cast of characters, his drinking buddies, that I'd met dozens of times before, and the same old man teasing would ensue, 'No way she's your daughter, Rock! She's way too pretty to be related to you.'"

"That's kinda funny, Mom, because you look just like him."

I certainly resemble the Sullivan side of the family and have repeatedly been told that I laugh and sound exactly like my dad's sisters. But, of course, I — healthy and sober — didn't look like the frail drunk guy in the baggy clothes who was perched on the corner barstool. What my dad had done to himself over the years made him unrecognizable as "one of us" to a passing stranger.

I continued my story for Kendall: "Getting away from my dad once we had nothing left to talk about proved challenging. Having more than my fill of awkward 'bonding time,' I would typically begin my exit strategy by explaining that I had just gotten into town and had other places and people to visit during my short stay. On the occasion that you came with me and were waiting patiently at Aunt Beth's house, I would use that tidbit as my excuse. That often backfired, though, because it opened the door for him to talk shit about Aunt Beth, who he also never visited despite her living only a few miles from the bar. 'You gonna see your sister? She lives down the goddamn street, and you'd think she'd bring her ass over here once in a while. She better never ask me for anything 'cuz she ain't gettin' my help!' The first few times I was on the receiving end of his tirade about Beth, I defended her and reminded him that perhaps instead of calling her names and demanding attention, he should step outside the damp, dark bar walls for once in his life and make an effort to spend time with her and his grandkids. When that had the opposite effect and resulted in more bitching and stories of his martyrdom, I switched tactics and eliminated getting dragged further into the conversation by saying, 'Well, I gotta get moving. See ya, Rock,' as I swiftly headed out the door."

Each of these "hometown tour" conversations with Kendall took place in the car. We'd pull into parking lots and driveways or idle the car along the curb on the street out front, but I never gave the slightest hint that I wanted to get out of the car and take her for a walk around or inside any of these old haunts. I think she understood this implicitly — that we were "safe" from my past if we stayed at a distance, inside the car, and watched it through the windshield like watching a sad movie on a screen.

Although I had traveled this road countless times throughout my life, it was eerily different this day — traveling with my daughter, and "coming home" in the wake of my father's death. Noticeably absent were the roiling balls of anxiety in the pit of my stomach. Instead, a sense of calm and resolve passed through me. It suddenly dawned on me, while navigating Rocky's daily bar crawl with my daughter riding shotgun (much like I had done my entire childhood with my mom behind the wheel), that I would never again be making that obligatory visit to The Riverside to see my dad.

Kendall and I weaved our way around Brooks Fountain and headed up Michigan Avenue before pulling into my sister's driveway. At last, we were there. I absolutely adored Beth's 1869 Italianate home, which was perfectly positioned within walking distance of all the cute shops downtown Marshall had to offer — specifically Louie's Bakery! She was living out our childhood dream of being "Townies," and I made sure to take full advantage of the perks of such an ideal location on every visit. Despite the somber reason for our unplanned October reunion, it was perfect timing because Beth — now an empty-nester — had just announced that she would be moving to Japan in a few short months to work for the Department of Defense as the Reading Specialist & Program Coordinator for Yokosuka Middle School, which was housed on our naval base. When the news of her gigantic solo adventure broke, I struggled with the realization that we would no longer have daily phone conversations, witty banter via text, nor continue to benefit from the meager four-hour drive between us. When we were little and only had each other to depend on in our chaotic home, we were best buds. Throughout the teenage years and into early adulthood, we despised one another and were repeatedly told by our mother that one day we'd only have each other to rely on — so we should appreciate having a sibling and "knock the hateful shit off." (She was, of course, right.) Fast forward to me becoming a mother, in need of Beth's big-sister advice on parenting, and we've been thick as thieves ever since — having supported each other through divorces, moves, family drama, and everything in between. So, the gravity of her leaving made me extremely sad, and I was intent on soaking up every minute of her still being stateside. My dad's death gave me an excuse to be here with her. There were silver linings everywhere I looked.

With the drive behind us and the purpose of the trip looming large, it was time to prepare for the funeral. It wasn't going to be easy, but luckily, we had each other. Managing to get through my dad's funeral and the inescapable task of dredging up painful memories to prepare the eulogies we were asked to deliver would be the hardest—but most poignant—moment we'd share together. Neither of us are procrastinators (quite the opposite, actually, as overachievers), but the task of writing those final, emotional words about our dad in two days' time was something neither of us were in a hurry to accomplish. Instead, Beth and I decided that giving Kendall a guided *walking* tour of our youth — punctuated by specific landmarks and anecdotes to accompany each one — would be a more meaningful and productive use of our time. Our first stop: Marshall Middle School.

Hazard Lights:

Ignoring What Hurts

"I can't wait for you to see the middle school, Kendall!" Beth and I both shouted out in unison. It's not just any old school. That auditorium is so special to me because it's where practically every event in Marshall was showcased, including our dance recitals. This place holds so many happy and significant memories from our youth. I couldn't help but wonder what it felt like to be Kendall — to be seeing her mom and her aunt taking a walk down "memory lane" and to be trying to imagine me as a young girl.

Beth was anxious to show us the current classroom where she was teaching, so after peeking into the auditorium, we headed to the third floor to find her domain. Upon entering Beth's classroom — which was home to our favorite teacher, Mrs. Huepenbecker, when we were students there — I felt a flood of emotions rush over me. That room served as my secret refuge for most of eighth grade (more on that to come). To my surprise, the beautiful pine bookcases and cabinetry that consumed an entire wall of the room stood firmly intact. As I approached the cabinet door and peered inside, I would swear I heard the faint whisper of Mrs. H's voice, *"I told you it would all be okay. I'm so proud of you."*

I must've been in a momentary daydream and didn't hear Kendall's question. She touched my arm and repeated herself. "Mom, is this the teacher who taught you to journal?"

I smiled and nodded before answering: "Wow, good memory, Sis. Yes, she provided each student a journal at the beginning of the year, and one afternoon a week she gave us a 30-minute window to write about whatever we wanted, and we turned them in afterward. She would read them and write a short note back to each of us before handing the journals back the following week. I think I also told you that initially I hated it and wrote maybe two sentences of nonsense about clouds or the grass outside — because the rule was that we had to write something. Despite me being a brat about the assignment, Mrs. H always responded with kindness and showed genuine interest in what I said. She was a master at breaking down my walls and getting to the root of what was bothering me."

"Did you tell her about your dad always yelling at you or that he drank all the time?"

"Yeah," I said to her, with Beth standing at a distance and listening quietly. "A few months into the school year, I did begin mentioning things about my dad in the journal, which is when I learned that she also had experience living with an alcoholic. From then on, I had to learn to write really fast, because 30 minutes of journaling time was never enough for all the things I wanted to tell her!"

This tradition is one that I passed down to my daughter when the time was right. Inspired by Mrs. H and attempting to bring my best to the venture of parenting, I used journaling as a tool when Kendall was in the 4th grade and struggling with anxiety and expressing her feelings verbally. I suggested we keep a "Mom and Sis" journal. I would write a note to her, usually about how proud I was of something she said or did, or I'd give her a compliment about what an incredible kid she was, and I would leave it on her bed for her to find when she got home from school. She would then respond by telling me about something positive (or tough) about her day. She thought it was fun to "sneak" the journal into my room each night, placing it on my pillow for me to find later that evening. We went back and forth doing this for a full year until she found her voice and became more comfortable talking about her feelings than writing them down. I saved that journal and look back at it occasionally, silently thanking Mrs. H for the brilliant idea.

Beth pointed out a few more key spots within the middle school before we'd had our fill of the empty building and ventured off downtown, toward our old dance studio, then visited Brooks Fountain. I was mostly quiet as we walked, still thinking back on my 13-year-old self. With several blocks to continue our conversation, Kendall asked, "Did you guys just get used to how your dad treated you? I mean, were you able to ignore him and not let it bother you?"

I looked at Beth and smiled. "Let me take this one first, then you chime in."

The entire time we lived in that house, it felt like we were walking on eggshells. We lived in fear of setting Rocky off simply by breathing and existing. For some reason, my body responded particularly hard to stress and anxiety, I guess because my coping strategy was to bottle it up inside. Back when we were teenagers, mental health struggles were not as openly acknowledged, understood, or managed as they are today. Never wanting my dad to see or think he got to me, I held tightly to my tears, feelings and emotions, choosing to internalize his insults and rants rather than seek reassurance and comfort from anyone. Somehow, I managed to deal with his meanness without ever finding a healthy way to cope. I always walked into school, jobs, or public settings with a huge smile on my face or a joke to tell, careful not to share even a hint of the pain or sadness I felt inside.

I was never directly told to lie about our family, but based on my mom's actions and dedicated denial, it was an unspoken obligation I felt to continue — pretending we were a normal, happy family. The very opposite was the truth. My dad was an abusive drunk and a complete jerk 99.9% of the time. I didn't want anyone to know that, deep inside, I was struggling to ignore his demeaning insults and was absorbing more than I wished to admit. Learning to cope and handle any shit thrown my way without relying on anyone was an early defense mechanism I established, which served me well … until it didn't.

Doing my best to help Kendall understand what it was really like, I told her, "Aunt Beth and I got into trouble for making any sort of racket at home. I was an energetic kid who loved school and hanging out with friends. Like you, Kendall, I would get upset if I was too sick to go to school because I never wanted to miss anything. However, around the age of 13, it appeared that I was spending more of the school day in the nurse's office than in the classroom. I always had stomach issues that were too distracting to remain at school, so despite my begging to stay, I was always instructed by the school nurse to call my mom to pick me up. This royally pissed off Nana — not because she didn't care that I was sick but because her job as a court reporter in Juvenile Court only allowed for so many paid sick days, and I had damn near exhausted her allotment for the year within a three-month span. Although it was annoying and could get her in trouble at work, she always believed me and came. But, after many months of this happening, she told me we weren't going home but instead to our family physician, Dr. Jim Dobbins's office. Despite my begging for her to just take me home, she insisted that we figure out what was wrong with me."

I continued, looking at Kendall, "Now, I'm not saying you've ever called me to come get you from school when you weren't really sick," Kendall's head and eyes darted down, looking directly at her shoes as a smirk graced her face, "but anytime I truly didn't feel well at school, miraculously, the minute after Nana was called, I started to feel better. I knew I wasn't faking, but where did my stomachache go and why was I no longer feeling shaky or light-headed? I kept thinking, 'Holy hell, what if she takes me to the doctor, and he says there's nothing wrong with me? My mom will surely kill me.' Well, I guess that particular day, I'd find out the truth."

I was honestly shocked when Dr. Dobbins diagnosed me with a stress-induced stomach ulcer. Back then, doctors still thought ulcers were primarily caused by stress, so whatever gastrointestinal dysfunction I was actually experiencing got chalked up to an "ulcer," and we were told to treat it with dietary and lifestyle changes. On the one hand, I was relieved that there was medical evidence to prove I wasn't a faker; on the other, I was freaking out because what 13-year-old child is under the amount of stress and anxiety required to generate an ulcer? Being that there wasn't a lot that could be done aside from altering the acidity in my diet, getting ample rest, and finding better coping strategies, I was forced to learn how to better manage my feelings by talking through them and writing about them instead of internalizing them. Certainly, Rocky wasn't going to get sober to help his kid heal from her trauma-related GI pain. As always, it was on me to "figure it out."

"So that's how journaling in that class helped you feel better?"

"It definitely helped a lot," I explained, "but Mrs. H went above and beyond to help me. After learning what the doctor said — because of course I wrote about it — I came into school the next week to find that Mrs. H, the best homeroom teacher in history, had prepared a 'Laurie cabinet,' as she called it. She had emptied out the contents of one of her pine storage cupboards and stocked it full of cranberry juice and sleeves of saltine crackers in case my nausea or cramping flared up. It was our little secret. Whenever I arrived at school with a stress-induced upset stomach, likely because of my dad's morning screaming, I would head straight for Mrs. H's cupboard of remedies, and she would write a note for me to take to whichever of the other classes (e.g., science, math, social studies) I was tardy to. I also began scheduling twice-monthly appointments with the school counselor who, after much resistance on my part, was also able to cut through my fake smile to get to the deeper issues weighing me down.

It felt good to talk to my daughter about my childhood and to show her the places where I struggled and learned, suffered and endured. As the three of us approached Brooks Fountain and found a bench to sit on, Beth gave me a break from the emotional storytelling and launched into her specific memories and takeaways of living with my dad, which although we lived in the same house, were in many ways drastically different from mine. Unintentionally, I zoned out and was reminded of some of the tougher aspects of that particular age, none of which I felt comfortable sharing with Kendall.

In 1989 — the year my father nearly choked my mother to death — I was suffering greatly from post-traumatic stress disorder (PTSD) and what I know *now* to have been undiagnosed anxiety and depression. Among the frequent thoughts I wrestled with at that time were that maybe everything my dad was saying about me was true. Would this world and my family be better off if my worthless, dumb ass were no longer in it? Several times,

I threatened to run away, even placing my packed bag near the front door to let my parents know I was serious. But with each feeble attempt, their response was laughter and wishing my six-, nine-, and eleven-year-old self the best of luck in the big world out there. Clearly, no one took me seriously. But at age 13, my emotions in overdrive, I recall my dad berating me for an hour and calling me every hurtful name imaginable before ordering me to go to my room, all because I failed to tightly seal a container in the refrigerator, which could've spoiled the food had he not corrected my stupidity.

I remember that moment in my life in such detail. I stayed awake that entire night and contemplated the various ways I could end my life. All I truly wanted was an escape from the torture and mental abuse, but I was convinced this was the only option. I suppose I'm grateful that we didn't own guns, that none of us took prescription medications, and that Google didn't exist for me to search for alternative suicide methods, because if any of those things had been at my disposal, I'm not sure I'd have made it another day.

Grateful that such an impulsive thought never amounted to a disastrous end, I instead found a more passive way to handle my feelings or emotions and avoid acknowledging them through the use of two simple words: *I'm fine.*

Those words have become a conditioned response that I've always defaulted to for the entirety of my life, no matter the situation. If I'm served cold food that tastes dreadful, when asked about my meal, I let the server know that, "It's fine, thank you." Someone terribly hurts my feelings? Again, I overlook my sadness or anger and reply, "It's okay, I'm fine." Honestly, what does that even mean and why is it so damn hard to admit that I am not always fine? Perhaps it's the confrontation I'd prefer to avoid, which is why I was conditioned to just deal with my dad's bullshit internally and keep my mouth shut. I was trained to keep a megawatt grin plastered on my face and fake my way through it. After all, that had been my default response every day of my life, regardless of the circumstance … so why change now?

I know that living this way is mentally and physically disruptive, but I've found it extremely tough to change deep-rooted behaviors ingrained in you for a lifetime. Recently, a colleague of mine told me that she thinks of the word "fine" as an acronym that stands for "feelings inside not expressed" — FINE. And that really struck a chord with me. Every time I've said, "I'm fine," what I'm really saying is that I don't feel safe or capable of expressing my feelings, so I don't. But I'm learning and growing, and embracing the truth that "it's okay not to be okay." And once again, motherhood served as the catalyst I needed to inspire meaningful change in how I think, feel, behave, and speak.

A hard reality suddenly hit me one day during a routine interaction with Skyler that required an immediate course correction with how I parent my children and honor myself. Over the years, I've continually repeated the same phrases to them: "You're okay" — to minimize any potential overreaction when they hurt themselves or "Everything will be fine" — when something doesn't go their way. I was unknowingly dismissing their feelings and inadvertently teaching them to hide how they really felt, like I'd always done.

On a chilly afternoon in mid-December 2022, Skyler had his first visit to Arami Acres, a local non-profit farm that provides therapeutic horse riding to individuals with disabilities, and he appeared very anxious the entire drive there. His reaction to the unfamiliar surroundings and uncertainty about what he would be required to do while there was not unlike every other time he's presented with a new experience or environment, so I reminded him that there were absolutely no expectations, and he could take all the time he needed to become comfortable in the arena and around the horses. Upon arrival, Skyler cautiously placed one foot into the sand-filled riding arena, only to immediately lift it right back out and beeline for the exit. Seeing the panicked expression on his face, I attempted to calm him by softly repeating the words, "You're okay," "You're fine," and "No need to worry," which didn't help reduce his level of anxiety one bit. After a few minutes, we retreated to our car, undeterred and committed to trying again soon. On the drive home, I began replaying years of scenarios like this in my mind, where my attempts to calm and comfort Skyler in times of distress appeared to actually make him more agitated. *Did he not trust me to keep him safe?* I dissected every action and reaction, trying to crack the communication code represented by Skyler's nonverbal, physical cues. Then, it hit me, like Skyler so often does (c'mon, that's funny!) ... it's because he's *not* fine! The more I thought I was reassuring him, the more irritated he became. What I believed was helpful to Skyler was the exact opposite, and I was oblivious to it, until now.

As parents, we do and give what we *know* — based on how we were raised and what we've learned along the way. But we never stop growing or evolving throughout our lifetime — and when we know better, we do better. So, on our next trip to the farm, I implemented an entirely new mindset. The moment we got out of the car, and I saw Skyler's apprehension take hold, I addressed him in this way, "Buddy, it looks like you are feeling scared about approaching the horses, and that makes sense. If you want, you can take my hand and lead me to the arena at your own pace. You decide what you feel comfortable doing, okay?" He paused in place, taking in my words before reaching out to grab my hand. Skyler led me to the arena and slowly walked through the thick layer of sand toward Olivia, the horse chosen specifically for him. He extended two fingers and briefly stroked the bridge of Olivia's nose. It was one of the most emotional moments of my parenting journey so far, for a multitude of reasons. It's always amazing to me that not only does Skyler understand every word I say (which is an argument I've had with medical experts and therapists for his entire life), but for a person unable to explain or express his feelings and emotions with words, he always acknowledges when I've gotten something right by responding with his body. He finally felt heard *and* understood. After almost a year of weekly visits to the barn, Skyler, at his own pace, excelled and now willingly sits atop Olivia's saddle *and* rides her around the arena. Had I kept insisting that he was "fine" when he wasn't fine, we might never have come to this incredible place.

I often wish Skyler could just tell me what he was thinking and feeling, and that it didn't have to take months or years to interpret his body language for possible answers. However, it's often that each puzzle I solve with Skyler leads to equally applicable lessons for how I show up as a mother for Kendall, too. It's as if God prefers that I discover these valuable teachable moments in the intended way — from my first born.

Just as with Skyler, my default position when something disappointing or unexpected happened with Kendall was to tell her, "It's going to be fine." While I truly believe that most of the time things work out exactly as they should, as God planned, that mindset doesn't provide much comfort or take the sting away from an upsetting situation.

Not long after my revelation at the barn, the time had come for Kendall to begin applying for college scholarships. Understanding the lofty requirements and stiff competition due to numerous applicants for each award, she set her sights on winning enough to pay for her entire first year of college, if not more. Academically, she was among the top 5 in her large, senior class and is also a talented writer, so generating a well-crafted essay and meeting the GPA standards were the least of her concerns. The one area she was significantly lacking was in community service and volunteer hours, but she captured the many examples she did have and hoped for the best. As the months passed, and Kendall learned that she had been admitted to all the colleges she applied to (her top choices being expensive, out-of-state schools), she grew more anxious for the various scholarship winners to be announced. The time finally came and to her dismay, emails and letters arrived daily with the same canned response, "Due to the abundance of highly qualified applicants, we regret to inform you …" I'm sure you can fill in the rest. She became more devastated and angrier with each rejection, taking it all very personally. Before I could do or say anything, Kendall looked at me and said, "It's fine, Mom. I don't care," but of course I knew that was not at all true.

My heart broke into tiny pieces. To her surprise, I didn't let that statement of dismissal conclude our discussion, nor did I raise my voice or allow her to storm off, as was usually the case. Instead, I reassured her that it's okay to be upset or disappointed and encouraged her to share with me how she's truly feeling instead of bottling it up. In addition, I promised Kendall that allowing herself to express emotions in the moment rather than silently internalizing them is a much healthier way to process and cope during challenging times. With that, her body language and demeanor quickly shifted, eyes filled with tears, and what followed was a much deeper conversation about all that had been weighing her down, specifically the pressure she continually placed on herself to be perfect and never fail.

I owe so much to Skyler and Kendall for teaching me important lessons about being a better parent —one who observes and listens rather than ignores and dictates. Much of what I've learned from my children has transformed how I now live my own life and has made me a much better version of myself. Quickly fading is the "fake it with a smile" mentality that got me through my childhood and early adulthood. I no longer wear a façade, pretending that I'm never frustrated, angry, or worried about the unknown. If you ask how I'm doing now, be prepared, because if things have been rough, I'll be sharing the truth. I'm done pretending I'm fine.

Body Shop:
Confronting Our Generational Trauma

Beth, Kendall, and I concluded the literal "skeleton tour" through downtown Marshall (every October, local businesses decorate a collection of skeletons according to a specific theme), and Beth suggested dinner at The Stagecoach Inn, so she and Kendall could enjoy the best cheeseburger in mid-Michigan. After some teasing from both about my refusal to consume red meat since the age of 10, I was reminded of a few specific childhood moments that contributed to my ongoing negative self-talk and my struggle to love and appreciate myself.

"Kendall, did you know your mom was nicknamed 'shrimp' because she was always small and a picky eater?" Aunt Beth teased.

"Clearly, she's still that way, since she won't eat red meat and it seems like everything else upsets her stomach."

"Shut it, Bennie," I snapped back at my sister. "Do you want to tell Kendall the story of how you got *that* nickname?"

"I would be *happy* to share the story," Beth said, jumping at the chance to make sure Kendall heard the accurate version. "Kendall, I'd had beautiful, long, blonde hair until the summer before 4th grade, when my mom decided it was too difficult to take care of. Despite the detangler she used, it was still difficult to comb through my hair when it was wet, and I cried after every bath. So, to the hair salon we went, my hair in a ponytail — for the last time in a long time. I think her name was Dee, the woman who butchered my hair and destroyed my young life by loosening the ponytail slightly and then cutting it off. Every attempt was made, I'm sure, to make it look cute, but it was short. Really short. I was 9 years old, with glasses and a retainer cemented to my teeth, so this short haircut just added to an already awkward-looking kid."

Beth was deep into her story, and Kendall was eating it up. Beth continued: "Anyhoo, cut to a craft show (Nana and Aunt Sandy were vendors), and because our dad was usually at the bar all day on Saturdays, our choice was to be dragged to the bar or dragged to the craft show. We chose the craft show because at least there were things to see and better snacks to eat. We'd nickeled and dimed our mom all day that day and she finally relented and allowed me to buy a hot dog from a food truck at the event. I'm sure I was wearing a t-shirt and blue jeans, and I'm also sure no one had made my hair look 'cute,' because after ordering that hot dog, the old man (who I maintain had to have been nearsighted) asked, 'What's your name, little boy?' Horrified, I barked out, 'Beth!' — but when you've got a retainer-induced speech impediment and an old man who was also likely hard of hearing, things went sideways quickly. 'What's that? Ben?' I paid for the hot dog and ran, crying, back to my mom's booth. Of course, *your* mom overheard the story and started calling me Bennie, which then got me to calling her Larry. But *my* nickname stuck. And eventually, I grew out my hair."

And even though she still sounds bitter about the incident, I lovingly still call her Bennie even now. It's a term of endearment, really.

Kendall, not having a sister of her own, was getting a sense of what it's like to have two girls in one family — the built-in friendship, the bickering, the teasing. I wanted to revisit a topic that had come up before the Bennie story, so I interjected: "Let's get back to my pickiness, shall we? It was as much about hating the taste or smell of certain foods as it was their textures. I couldn't stand peanut butter and jelly sandwiches because I hated any foods to touch one another. In fact, Thanksgiving dinner practically gave me nightmares because if the green bean juice bled into my mashed potatoes or bits of stuffing landed in my salad, I lost my mind. The mere scent of tomato soup made me gag, and the fact that our babysitters always served grilled cheese with tomato soup at least once a week really pissed me off. And applesauce, yeah, I'll pass. Gross."

Let's just say that I was very "selective" about the foods I allowed onto my plate, and at the ripe old age of 10, decided that I would no longer consume red meat — which is something I've held firmly to throughout the past 39 years. I made this decision mainly due to how disgusting raw meat looked and the fact that packaged meat (e.g., hotdogs and bologna) were made from "leftover parts" of slaughtered pigs made my decision an easy one to make. Being that strong-willed when it came to food got me in loads of trouble, particularly with my dad. I distinctly recall the "Broccoli Incident of 1980" being one of my earliest protests. Beth was done with her dinner and had left the table, and of course my dad wasn't home to eat with us. My mom told me that I could not leave the table until I ate *all* the broccoli on my Tom & Jerry plastic plate, to which I eventually bargained down to eating only half of the portion originally given to me. I would swear an hour went by, and the broccoli on my plate remained untouched. I refused to budge. My mom didn't get angry very often, but after realizing I was never going to eat that stupid broccoli, she got the angriest look on her face and yelled that it was almost bedtime, and I had five more minutes to eat what was now a cold, limp, green slug on my plate or else. Still refusing to touch it, let alone eat it, less than five minutes later, I declared my hunger strike a victory as she ordered me to go to my room.

Kendall appeared amused as I recounted these stories. Her smile was all I needed to keep going. I continued: "Moving on ... The choice to exclude red meat from my diet was a pretty big deal, Kendall, considering my dad, who worked as a salesman for Swift-Eckrich, a packaged meat company, expected every home-cooked dinner prepared by Nana to include meat and potatoes. We always found it comical that he dictated what dinner had to be but rarely came home before midnight to eat it. But I digress. Our refrigerator was always packed full of Swift-Eckrich products: hot dogs; bratwurst; bologna; cold cuts and olive loaf — seriously, what the hell else excites the taste buds as much as olives and pimentos jammed into sliced bologna? Gross! With those selections as our main lunch options and with dinners that featured pork chops, steak, spaghetti and meatballs, pot roast, beef stew, or meatloaf, what was I supposed to eat? On the rare night my dad was home for dinner and Nana tried to make me a cheese sandwich, Kraft Macaroni & Cheese, Spaghetti-o's, or a can of Campbell's ABC vegetable soup instead of what everyone else was eating, he would holler, 'She'll eat what we fix, or she'll eat nothing at all!' Fearful that I would never grow or worse, suffer the unlikely fate of starving to death, Nana would wait until my dad retired to the basement or left for the evening and then make my food.

"Besides just worrying about what we ate, Aunt Beth and I were never comfortable with our body shape or size. I'm not sure we would've fixated on it so much had our dad not body-shamed us so often. I remember always thinking I looked fat. It seemed that many of my dance costumes triggered my insecurities. I vividly recall crying in our hotel room while in Pigeon Forge, TN at a national dance competition because my jazz solo costume, a red unitard, made me look fat. All 65 pounds of me. Frustrated that I was going to make us late for my category, Nana said, 'Laurie, don't be ridiculous. You look fine. Now let's go.' And that was that.

"I'm sure I was only imitating what I'd witnessed my mom do countless times — critique her body head to toe in the full-length mirror that hung on her bedroom wall. She repeatedly would say, out loud, that she was 'fat' and needed to lose weight. What immediately followed would be another attempt for quick weight loss via some random fad diet. There was the Beverly Hills fruit-only diet, the cabbage-soup diet, and the cottage-cheese diet. There were also Jane Fonda workout videos and random exercise gadgets like the Thigh Master, Velcro ankle and wrist weights, and a stationary exercise bike — all overtaking the basement. Aunt Beth and I shared tons of giggles at Nana's expense — mimicking movements like the 'fire hydrant,' 'donkey kick,' or 'leg scissors,' alongside her as she exercised. As funny and innocent as it seemed at the time, I would say that it significantly impacted what I thought it meant to be pretty or appealing. Rocky's intentionally hurtful descriptions of our rear ends, while amusing to him, also added to our body insecurities."

My daughter interrupted my story. "Wait, hold up. What the heck is a Thigh Master?"

Beth and I figured the best way to answer Kendall's question was by using the power of the internet to show her the old commercial advertisements featuring Suzanne Somers. Kendall found them to be equally ridiculous and amusing.

When Beth and I were roughly ages 12 and 11, clearly old enough for chores, it was routine that the three "women" of the house cleaned up after dinner, while our dad, if he was around, would disappear to the basement to smoke cigarettes and continue drinking. Our mom always washed the dishes while Beth and I alternated responsibilities for who dried them and who put them away. Like clockwork, Dad would wander upstairs midway through our chore and over-dramatize his inability to walk past us through the narrow kitchen because our butts were too large for him to get by. He also nicknamed our asses "small, medium, and large," but we didn't dare ask him which size belonged to whom. He really found enjoyment in describing the width of our rear ends using an ax handle for reference. A common phrase would be "your ass is three ax handles across."

Looking at my daughter, clearly aghast at hearing this story, I said, "Now Kendall, you've seen all my scrapbooks with tons of pictures of me at that age. I was roughly 4 foot 6 inches tall and approximately 70 pounds — clearly not overweight and neither was Aunt Beth or Nana, but he sure had us believing we were obese!"

"I can't even imagine Josh telling me I looked fat or that I had a big butt. That's weird and mean," Kendall marveled.

This is why I've purposely avoided talking about dieting and weight with Kendall. I wanted to keep her from developing body-image issues and insecurities. Instead, what I've tried to teach her, which took me until my 30s to figure out, is that to truly love and appreciate your exterior, you need to be confident with who you are on the inside. By doing that, someone else's opinion about your appearance simply won't affect you. What *you* think of yourself is all that matters. I consider her current disinterest in social media, in wearing makeup, and in taking selfies — the outcome of which are so over filtered that they don't even resemble the actual person — a parenting job well done! I guess she does sometimes listen when I speak.

I seriously wish I could bottle Kendall's confidence, though. She's truly wise beyond her years and has certainly taught me a thing or two about loving myself.

Changing your mindset after deeming yourself unworthy and unlovable is not something that happens overnight. As I mentioned, it wasn't until my mid-30s, miserable in my first marriage and questioning every aspect of my life up to that point, that I finally decided to invest in myself. For the first time, I believed I was worth it. I began attending weekly therapy sessions to wade through the negative labels and demeaning self-talk playing loudly on a loop through my head (thanks, Dad, for that parting gift) and uncovered what was most important to me. I was desperate to recover from my childhood and become a confident adult and parent with a greater appreciation and love for myself. It was extremely important that I model a strong self-worth for my children and teach them one of the best takeaways I gained from therapy: You must learn to be selfish before you can be selfless.

In 2008, after 10 years of marriage to my first husband, I found myself at a crossroads. Was I willing to continue co-existing in a loveless relationship, or did I deserve the chance to be truly happy — either on my own or perhaps with someone better suited for me? Reflecting on the many times I begged my mom to divorce my dad, it still shocks me that, to this day, she doubles down on her reasoning for not walking away, insisting it was purely financial. She has repeatedly told Beth and me, "I know you always wanted me to divorce him, but I suffered through that horrific relationship, so you girls would have nice clothes, prom dresses, and so we could stay in our home, and you wouldn't have to grow up living in a tiny apartment." She perhaps unknowingly made it *our fault* that we lived with an alcoholic who verbally and emotionally abused us all and who physically abused my mom. "I stayed for you" is a guilt trip, if I've ever heard one, and one that is entirely unfair to place on any child.

In examining my own dysfunctional relationship with my first husband, I knew I had difficult decisions to make. And I refused to make the same mistake with my children that my mother had made with hers. I knew leaving my marriage was not only in our collective best interests but, more importantly, I needed to clearly demonstrate to my daughter that she should never just settle or "suck it up" because it may seem the easier road to take. You must love yourself enough to walk away from an unhealthy relationship.

Although my ex wasn't an alcoholic, he was neglectful as a husband and father. In many ways, I was parenting alone anyway, particularly with handling all of Skyler's extra needs. After suggesting couples' therapy to him, which he swiftly turned down, it was clear that divorce was the answer. Choosing to launch myself into single parenting with a three-year-old and a five-year-old was a frightening decision, but it's one I wish my mom had made when I was Kendall's age. It was hard and empowering, full of freedom and opportunity to finally be myself and be the best mother I could be.

In the years following my divorce, my confidence and self-esteem grew leaps and bounds. I reintroduced myself to the activities I once loved, like marathon running, and prioritized strengthening my mental and physical health. I was able to do this because I no longer had someone looking over my shoulder, telling me I was selfish for wanting to carve out a little "me time." While true acceptance of my body shape and size will likely always be a work in progress, implementing a healthier lifestyle made me not only feel better inside and out but led to some productive discussions with Kendall as she grew up. I've always tried to instill in her that food should be viewed as fuel and that exercise makes her body stronger, so she would not fall into the trap most young girls do of comparing herself to others and obsessing about diets and weight with the hopes of achieving an unattainable physique, all the while harboring a distorted image of her own body.

While I'm proud to have recognized the importance of investing in myself and worked hard to heal the decades-old wounds to my self-worth, the most eye-opening aspect to come out of my post-divorce come-back was the impact those positive changes had on my parenting. Being mentally strong and kind to myself translated into me being an infinitely better mother. I'm more patient and affectionate and better able to regulate the tone of our household, which makes challenging days (particularly with Skyler) much easier to manage.

Becoming a parent comes with great responsibility and requires copious amounts of unconditional love and unwavering support. My sincerest hope is that my children have always felt loved and supported by me and that I've modeled for them the importance of investing in themselves. I also pray that I've taught Kendall the importance of appreciating the body God gave her by smiling with pride at the beautiful reflection in the mirror rather than criticizing herself as I grew up doing.

Knowing better is doing better. This was one life lesson they needed to learn from me, not the other way around.

Rear View Mirror:
The Truth About Where I Come From

Our lunch at The Stagecoach Inn was as delicious and relaxing as I had hoped — a truly special respite for me, Beth, and Kendall on what was eventually going to be a bittersweet visit. It was the last stop on our late afternoon "tour" before heading back to Beth's house to begin the sad business at hand. Settling in at Beth's house, we revisited the topic of our eulogies and really struggled to come up with stories we might share about Rocky that didn't pertain to his temper or alcohol. It seemed a damn near impossible task. We would be gathering with our aunts and uncles the following night to review the plans for Rocky's service, so we hoped that perhaps visiting with them would help us uncover some redeeming qualities he possessed — some stories worthy of a memorial service. Having only recently met a handful of my dad's extended family and now knowing some of the history of my parent's dreadful marriage, Kendall asked us a very logical question, "How did Nana and your dad even end up together?"

Such a loaded question, but I was determined to answer it. I said, "Honestly Kendall, I don't know. Nana and our dad were raised in two completely opposite family dynamics. I remember finally asking Nana the same question when I was around the age of 15 because I was sick of my dad's attitude and bullshit tantrums. Why in the hell did she marry him? I needed to know."

Kendall's question prompted me to think back to a memorable day — a day when my own perspectives and maturity started differentiating me from the child victim who I *had been* with the survivor I was *about to become*. It was a Saturday afternoon. Like practically every other Saturday afternoon, my dad had picked a fight about something stupid, ranted and cussed at all of us who were home, and stormed out of the house so he could justify sitting at The Riverside for the remainder of the day. As Rocky's baby blue Lincoln Continental squealed out of the driveway, my mom sat unbothered in her recliner in our living room, reading a Danielle Steel romance novel. I think she loved reading those books to escape the reality of her difficult and tumultuous marriage. With my dad finally gone and peace in our house restored, I said, "Mom! Why in the hell did you marry him? Aren't you sick of living with such an asshole?"

As she lifted the pastel bookmark from the end table and tucked it deep within the pages of the book's fantasy world (an escape I had abruptly yanked her from), she let out a lengthy sigh. I was about to learn the full story of how my mess of a family was created.

My mom, Judy Peterson, before she was Judy Sullivan, had what appeared to be an idyllic upbringing — the type that 1950s television sitcoms were developed around. Our grandparents, Warren and Erna, raised five children with my mom sandwiched between two older brothers and two younger sisters. To put in perspective just how carefree and entertaining life was for these five kids, they had a frickin' pet donkey, affectionately named Pancho, and were encouraged to pursue any creative ideas they had, like setting up a carnival in their backyard (to which they sold handmade tickets to neighborhood friends). They were also taught, at a young age, important life lessons about inclusion and respect for all people, regardless of ethnicity or skin color, as frequently demonstrated by my grandparents' instinctive acts of kindness toward anyone and everyone within their community.

Sadly, all this childhood joy and innocence came to a screeching halt when my grandmother unexpectedly passed away in her sleep from a brain aneurysm. My mom was now motherless at only 12 years old. Obviously heartbroken, my grandpa was greatly concerned about how he would continue to parent five children, particularly three little girls, the youngest being just six, as a widower. However, it wasn't long before he remarried the only grandmother I'd ever known, Audrey, who was also a widow. Based on the stories and troubling memories recited by my mom, aunts and uncles, my grandpa's marriage to Audrey seemed more of a business arrangement than a loving relationship. All the fun and carefree activities were replaced with excessive chores and emotional abuse. Picture a British Ms. Hannigan from the Broadway musical *Annie*, and you get the idea. Out of respect for his new wife, my grandpa didn't interject, and he let her maintain control of the household, which was a crushing blow to his five children, particularly when Audrey made my mom and her little sisters quit their beloved dance lessons for no apparent reason. So, it was no surprise that the day after my mom graduated high school, she packed her bags and moved out. The incredible tragedy of losing her mother at such a young age would set into motion a plummeting of her self-esteem and a trajectory of poor decisions, like choosing my dad as her future spouse.

On the flipside, my dad was raised in an environment that was the opposite. Our Sullivan grandparents, Roger and Mary Kathryn, were blessed with seven children, which included a set of triplets, my dad being one of the three. Having a pregnancy with natural multiples was extremely rare in 1948, so news of the triplets — two identical girls and one boy — made the headline in all the local papers. The story would be revisited throughout the years, as they highlighted the babies all grown up, attending prom and graduation. The dynamic in my dad's large, Irish Catholic family, as I've heard through stories shared by my five aunts and one uncle, was tense and void of affection. My grandfather was often cold, distant, emotionally unavailable, and quite the alcoholic. I also know that my dad harbored serious resentment toward my grandfather for always being too busy with working two full time jobs to attend my dad's baseball games or frankly any of his kids' activities. He never doled out praise for anything his children accomplished, whether it be academic or athletic in nature. Instead, my grandfather constantly yelled and made my dad feel unimportant or that he was a pain in the ass. If this sounds familiar, it's because it is. I can now appreciate that my dad fathered us — me and Beth — in much the same way that he was fathered. They say that the apple doesn't fall far from the tree, and some of the apples in my family were bitter and rotten.

My paternal grandmother, on the other hand, was always smiling and loving, often dismissing her husband's negativity with a shrug and the statement "Now Rog …" when Roger was out of line. I deemed her a saint for putting up with her grumpy, often demeaning and dismissive WWII-veteran husband, who thought nothing of cursing out and being physically violent with his children, making inappropriate jokes and discriminating comments whenever and wherever he pleased, and flipping his grandchildren the bird as a greeting because he found it humorous. Trust me, I was the recipient of many a middle finger and never quite understood the joke. Clearly, witnessing a father disrespecting his wife and children daily left a permanent imprint on my dad and instilled in him that his sharp tongue — consisting largely of profanity and hurtful name-calling — was an acceptable way to address his own future family. In my father's defense, it was all he had ever known.

My parents' two-year courtship, if you can call it that, was riddled with so many red flags that at the time of hearing the story from my mother, I couldn't fathom why she didn't run for the hills. According to my mom's own account, my dad stood her up on the first, second, and third dates they had made (why she kept giving him multiple chances, I'll never understand), and when he finally graced her with his presence for a date, he showed up to her apartment with a case of beer in hand, saying he preferred they stay in versus going out. He could never be without alcohol or cigarettes and apparently was the jealous type who couldn't stand anyone glancing in the direction of his new girlfriend. My mom was never a smoker and has only ever been an occasional drinker, meaning one cocktail, and she was done. I suspect that knowing you will always be forced to assume the role of responsible, sober driver (because your husband is always going to be falling down drunk) would make it hard to ever relax or enjoy yourself. My mom married a proverbial "ball and chain," despite knowing from the start that he was a troubled young man with little to offer.

"After all of that, how could she marry him?" Kendall wisely questioned.

"Honestly, Aunt Beth and I never understood that, either. The bigger question we could never seem to get an answer to was why she *stayed* in that marriage for 25 miserable years! What makes us the saddest is that she 'tolerated' her marriage and, by doing so, allowed Aunt Beth and me to endure 18 years of abuse, too. Perhaps she hoped that one day my dad would change and learn to appreciate the amazing family he was missing out on. But that's not — at all — how things turned out."

I recounted for Kendall how the rest of that conversation went with my mom, sharing that after my mom finished her story about how they met and became a couple — and after I gave her grief about her poor decision-making — I swore, then and there, that I would never put up with a guy who treated me like that. My mom's only response was, "I certainly hope and pray you don't. If you've learned nothing else from me, I hope you never marry someone like your dad."

It really did make me sad to see the anguish in my mother's eyes and to hear in the undertone of her voice that she had essentially given up on ever living happily and growing old with someone who loved and respected her. All the years she's wasted trying to "fix him" took a huge toll on her self-worth, and it showed.

As we sat at Beth's house, telling old stories, I think we all knew that we'd have to shift gears soon to start planning the funeral. But there was something so "final" about that, and we instinctively kept delaying the inevitable. Beth and I recounted more stories for Kendall about how we entertained ourselves on weekends when Rocky was getting plastered, which most often entailed visiting the Lakeview Square Mall in Battle Creek, Michigan, and spending the night with friends — all of whom had fun households filled with laughter and togetherness, safety and peace. I repeatedly said back then — to myself and to others — that when I had a family of my own, our home would be where all the kids preferred to hang out.

Drive In:
Family Bonding as We Grieve

In my sister's living room that evening, Beth and I discussed reaching out to a couple childhood friends who were a big part of our lives back in the day and inviting them over the following night. "I love throwing an impromptu gathering," Beth said. "I'll make some snacks, and we can toast Rock and catch up with Aimee and Greg, Beth J., and Bob."

We filled Kendall in on our plan and told her a little bit about each of our friends who would be coming over, emphasizing that we'd known them since middle school.

"Did you ever have friends stay the night at your house? Since your dad was at the bar on weekends, he wouldn't be there to bother you, right?" She wondered.

Before social media was invented (I know, it's not lost on me that many of you reading this have never known a world without it), I experienced a painful form of envy when it came to my perspectives on other — functional — families. I remember enacting the comparison game inevitably brought on through observation when spending the night or hanging out with my friends' families, who all seemed so utterly "normal" and nice.

"Believe me, Kendall, we tried when we were older — like eighth grade into high school. We figured at that age; it would be less intimidating to our friends for our dad to come home drunk," I explained. "Beth and I were obviously used to the swearing and yelling, but there was no way to really prepare our friends for it. His antics scared them badly enough that it usually became the first and last time someone ever stayed over. It was humiliating. So, I took every chance I was offered to get out of there, too.

"I'll never forget one weekend in fifth grade, my friend Aimee, who you'll meet tomorrow night, invited me to a Saturday night sleepover, which Nana agreed to — with the understanding that she would be picking me up bright and early Sunday morning for church. It annoyed me that I was never allowed to sleep in and skip Mass occasionally, and that I had to pack clothes appropriate for church. But, considering I would be free from a drunken night of fighting at my house, I was grateful and willing to do it. Aimee's house was a revolving door for kids; it didn't hurt that she was a 'Townie,' and we could walk there after school. Her house was one of my favorite places to hang out. No matter if it was pizza in the living room or a home-cooked meal served at the dinner table, everyone joined together for the meal. That night, I recall we sat around their dining room table, and in stunned silence I observed Aimee, her two sisters, and their parents loudly laughing and teasing about what was going on at school (basically who was mad at who for that week and which boys we thought were cute) and sharing anything else on their minds while we ate. I think I was unsure of how to react to the freedom to speak. At our house, if my dad was actually home to eat dinner with us, and Aunt Beth or I even attempted to tell a 'what happened at school today' story while he read his newspaper during the meal, we would be glared at, told to shut our damn mouths, or be sent to our rooms."

I paused to gauge her reaction. "I can't even imagine you getting mad at me for talking to you."

"I know you're annoyed with me always asking about your day as soon as you get home from school or during dinner, but maybe now you understand why it's important to me? And, why it irritates me when you refuse to engage in conversation and your only answers are 'Fine' or 'I don't know?'"

She bit her bottom lip as she processed this intel and then said, "Makes sense. Sorry, Mom."

I winked and nodded, saying, "It's okay, Sis. To put it mildly, Kendall, dinners were the source of great anxiety for Aunt Beth and me, which is why dinner at Aimee's seemed so abnormal compared to what I was used to. Good, but weird and new to me."

Following dinner at Aimee's, all those years ago, I helped clear the dishes from the table, as my mother had raised me to do, and I asked Aimee in all seriousness, "Was tonight a normal dinner at your house?"

I knew just by the look she gave me in response that my question was strange, and I suddenly felt awkward and exposed. Confused, she replied, "I don't understand what you mean?"

I told her to forget it, and we went to her room. At that moment, I realized that *our* house wasn't normal, and I couldn't possibly invite friends over. I thought about how traumatizing it would be for someone to experience a single night — or even a single hour — of my life.

On nights we weren't at the dance studio, my mom would cook dinner while we did our homework. If my dad came home directly after work, since his office was two miles down the road, we could expect dinner to be served somewhere between 5:30 and 6:30 p.m. Beth and I were conditioned to be silent during dinner anytime he planned to grace us with his presence. His routine never changed. The *Jackson Citizen Patriot* newspaper lay next to his plate, and he would begin reading it as he started with a salad (we always had salad) topped off with cottage cheese and French dressing. (Gross.) If one of us dared to speak, he would glare directly at the offender and holler that he was "trying to read the goddamn paper." Sometimes that comment was enough to shut down the small talk, and he stayed at the table for the entire meal. The other variation would result in him picking up his paper and salad and retreating to the basement "to eat in peace," eventually followed by a demand for somebody to deliver his dinner to a TV tray down there.

It wasn't only conversation that pushed him downstairs. It could also be silverware. One accidental scraping of a knife or fork on the plate resulted in a fist pounding on the table to scare the shit out of us, which ultimately was counterproductive because, at that point, my hands would've been shaking and much more likely to scrape the plate again. The real stare downs and perfectly executed insults, though, generally came with dessert a few hours after dinner.

While we cleared the table and took our respective positions at the sink — washing, drying and putting away the dishes as quietly as possible — my dad would momentarily relax, watching the evening news and enjoying several post-meal cigarettes. Instinctively, as the last dish was placed into the cabinet, he would yell out, "_____ (insert 'Beth' or 'Laurie' here), bring me some ice cream!" Typically, as pre-teens, Beth and I would play a quick game of rock, paper, scissors to see who was stuck with the chore of serving his ungrateful ass, but a few times when we were elementary age, and our mom still held out hope for family bonding, she used his demand for dessert as an opportunity. She prepared four bowls of ice cream — Butter Pecan for my dad, his favorite, and Neapolitan (chocolate, vanilla, and strawberry) for the rest of us and we would attempt to watch television together. I seriously would like to meet a person who has mastered the art of eating anything in a ceramic bowl with a metal utensil and not making a sound. For the rest of us mere mortals, it's damn near impossible. But according to my dad's dramatic outburst — which involved cursing and references to a pig digging through a trough — I broke the sound barrier the moment my spoon clanged against my bowl and, apparently, I did it on purpose to piss him off.

My entire life, I never understood what made my dad so angry — so quick to yell or make threats, so volatile and fragile like a bomb. I didn't know why he drank so much and so consistently, but when I grew up, I would learn that he'd been drinking and smoking to excess since he was 13, often vomiting booze over the side of the top bunk bed he shared with his brother. What kind of trauma had he endured that he wanted so desperately to numb the pain with alcohol and rage? For all the ways in which I feared and hated him, I always wanted him to be a good person. Today, I wonder if he once *was* a good person, a sweet little boy — and if he could have been a good husband and father, even, had his own young life unfolded differently. Days from his funeral, I found myself secretly wanting to ask him: "What happened to you, Rocky? Who hurt you?" It would be years later before I would find out.

Beth and I used to compare notes about the families of our friends and sometimes we even included TV sitcom families like the Keatons of *Family Ties* or the Seavers of *Growing Pains*, often based on the likability and involvement of the dad, and we'd fantasize we had a family like that. Of course, even the fun dance dads, silly jokester dads, and homework-helping dads we knew (and had put on a pedestal) likely had their flaws, too. But as a middle school kid dealing with an absentee, alcoholic, and abusive dad, it was hard not to envy the kids who seemed blessed with the perfect father we so desperately wanted. My desire to trade places with kids who seemingly won the lottery on dads made me sad and angry with God for selecting this paternal nightmare for me. What did Beth and I do to deserve this?

While I don't envision that God is in heaven playing a random game of "Duck, Duck, Goose" as His way of selecting how children and their future parents will be matched, I do believe God perfectly places people, specifically children, into our lives quite purposefully. Maybe my sister and I were specifically chosen for our parents, but at this point in my life and parenting journey — at the time of writing and publishing this book — I believe His plan was intended to prepare us for our own future children He'd selected.

When you're born into a fractured family, it's nearly impossible to single-handedly create a connection within your household when each member is not fully invested. My parents lived separate lives, had absolutely nothing in common, and tolerated one another while coexisting under the same roof. My father admittedly never wanted to marry or have children, and yet he did, without explanation. Like his drinking, "family life" was a place where Rocky hid from whatever demons were haunting and chasing him. Yet he found happiness and peace nowhere.

There were no specific moments, consistent routines, or annual traditions allocated as "family time" where the four of us — Mom, Dad, Beth, and I — gathered to spend quality time with one another. I'm also confident no one ever expected an RSVP for four from our family; however, my mom always felt it necessary to make excuses for Rocky's absences (and by excuses, I mean lie and lie some more). "Rocky isn't feeling well and is sorry he can't be here." "Rocky had to work late and couldn't make it." Hearing those falsehoods over and over really irritated me. I used to ask my mom why she chose to enable his poor choices instead of being honest, but I don't recall her having a clear answer for me. I assume, after all those years of parenting solo, it was just easier for her to give an autopilot response, even when people quit asking or caring why my dad wasn't there. He was the bad guy, but she covered for him all those years.

Even as I look back through photo albums documenting my birth through high school graduation, very few memories, significant events, or random snapshots include Rocky. Those photos certainly don't reflect any family bonding. The smiles on our faces suggest we were happy, and I'm sure we were on Christmas mornings, birthdays, and dance recitals. But behind every one of those special moments is what happened later … after a six-pack or so of beer. And *that* is what *we* remember when we look at those pictures, not what presents we got or how special the day might have started out. We have never discussed what happened after many of those pictures were taken because my mom refused to engage in those conversations. Her only addiction was denial.

Because we didn't really have family traditions or much fun at all in my childhood home, I made it a priority, both as a single mom and then as a family of four with Josh, to create those bonds and meaningful moments with Skyler and Kendall. While our family dynamic may appear drastically different than I once envisioned and daydreamed about, given Skyler's serious special needs, our version of "normal" has been a blessing and allowed a closeness to develop between us that would benefit me at least as much as it has benefitted my kids.

To be frank, this was not always my perspective. Learning to let go so that I could grow was an important lesson about acceptance, which I have both Skyler and Kendall to thank. They helped me understand that my past is behind me and that the future is now, with them and with Josh.

While I desperately wanted to be the mom who complained about (but secretly loved) having to travel every weekend to sporting events my kids participated in, to have the house with a revolving door of kids coming for playdates and sleepovers, and to be the referee when my kids' nonstop teasing about each other's boyfriends and girlfriends or arguing about whose turn it was to use the car, that has never been my reality. Instead, our household is much quieter, and rarely will you find anyone other than the four of us inside.

It wasn't always that way, at least where Kendall was concerned. I recall her 7th birthday party being quite a big deal. This would be Kendall's first party and sleepover combination. I allowed her to invite seven girls, which I realize now was a ridiculously large number of children for a first overnight, but Josh, my boyfriend at the time, agreed to help me supervise them all. As each of her friends entered our house, Kendall innocently announced, "My brother has 'the autism' and likes to pull hair. So, you should probably stay away from him."

I was mortified and dismissed her comments with promises that no one would get hurt or lose any hair on my watch. As the girls were getting settled, lining up sleeping bags and putting on PJs, Josh, sensing my concern with what the girls were thinking about Skyler, immediately sprang into action. He scooped up tiny 9-year-old Skyler and started chasing the girls around the house. They squealed and laughed while Skyler giggled and clapped overhead, bouncing up and down on Josh's hip as he zig-zagged between the furniture, pretending to come close to catching them. Potential crisis averted, and fun was had by all.

Kendall hosted a few more sleepovers after that, but once out of elementary school, she no longer had interest in inviting anyone over — even after school for a few hours. I repeatedly asked her if it had anything to do with Skyler and, if so, I'd be happy to keep him completely away from her friends, but she always dismissed that as the possible reason and said nothing more. Fast forward to high school, and I figured the fact that we had a swimming pool would be of great interest to Kendall and her friends, but she again refused to bring anyone over. Not only that, but when she made the firm decision both junior and senior years to not attend the homecoming dance or prom, I was an emotional wreck.

Knowing that Skyler will never host sleepovers, gather friends at our house or attend societal rites of passage like high school formal dances, it really devastated me that Kendall preferred isolating herself alone in her room instead of enjoying and appreciating the opportunity to make memories with peers, the likes of which Skyler cannot. I just couldn't understand (or accept) the fact that Kendall chose a different path from the traditional one, because it's one that felt completely unfamiliar to me. And truthfully, I was angry and felt robbed of the chance to bond with my kids over the few good childhood memories I could share with them — high school sports and activities, socializing and getting into mischief with my friends, etc. But now that she's graduated high school, I'll never be able to.

As I've said, learning to accept that Kendall is a completely different person than I was at her age has been a challenging concept to grasp. As much as I want her to find value or be interested in the same things I enjoyed, I now recognize that as much as I wanted those dress shopping, hair and nail appointments, and prom photo moments with her, it's not about me.

By letting go of my expectations and unrealistic vision of how our family dynamic should look, I have learned to appreciate the organic family bonding, rich in our own unique traditions and inside jokes, that was developing right under my nose. It's likely that the episodes of *Wheel of Fortune* we've watched every weeknight since the kids were little played a critical role in Skyler taking so quickly to his Spelling to Communicate program and helped Kendall perfect her quick wit. (I mean who hasn't poked fun at the contestants who terribly bumble when solving a puzzle?) It's heartwarming to know the entire staff of Skyler's favorite restaurant, Tucker's, is waiting to greet him by name every Saturday afternoon, and they are worried enough to call us if we don't show up. It's through our enjoyment of ridiculous reality television shows (cue *Toddlers and Tiaras, Dance Moms,* and *Married at First Sight*) along with all things HGTV and Food Network (House Hunters and Cupcake Wars are big favorites) that I've found the many things Kendall and I do have in common — a love for interior design, baking and real estate, and a fascination for people willing to make fools of themselves on national TV.

Instead of God giving me what I deemed a "perfect" family, He blessed me with what I needed — a meaningful relationship with both of my children that I didn't have with my dad and don't really have with my mom. Similarly, He provided Skyler and Kendall with the dad I wish I'd had. They certainly hit the dad lottery with Josh. Our family of four is beautiful beyond anything I could have imagined and is worth so much more than homecoming and prom pictures.

As the evening at Beth's wound down, our own scrapbooks and photo albums littering the living room carpet and providing the perfect illustration for our stories, Beth's cell phone rang. Following a brief conversation, she returned to the living room and said, "It was Mom. She invited the three of us to lunch tomorrow afternoon at Grand River Brewery," which was a two-minute walk from Beth's house. Beth and I exchanged familiar glances, always knowing what the other was thinking simply from a look (a sort of sister mind-synchronization we've always possessed), before I asked, "Do you think she's planning to tell us whether she's coming to the funeral or not?"

Attending the funeral of an ex-spouse and the parent of your children is a complicated issue, no matter how you cut it. At the time of my dad's death, my parents had been divorced for 24 years and lived entirely separate lives, despite the fact that my mom settled in a city just 15 minutes away from Marshall. Prior to getting into town, I'd heard through the grapevine that my mom had changed her mind and decided *not* to attend my dad's burial service. I had a lot of (mixed) feelings. Maybe she really *wasn't* coming to the funeral, but she hadn't yet revealed that little tidbit of information directly to us.

Up to this point, Kendall had been on the receiving end of countless stories, and it was equal parts therapeutic and emotionally draining for me — having to revisit all the trauma I thought no longer bothered me. After hearing Beth's reaction and my reaction to our mom potentially ditching the funeral, Kendall appeared confused and asked, "How long ago did Nana finally divorce your dad? I mean, after how he treated you guys, I get why she wouldn't want to go, but wouldn't she want to be there with you?"

See, even a 15-year-old gets the point. I obliged her and shared my memory of their dramatic divorce, which I had had a front-row seat to and which, up to this point, even Beth had only heard bits and pieces of due to her estrangement from my mom back then. I was 20 years old and away at college when my parents split. And while I had spent my entire life wanting my mom to escape and wanting my parents to stop torturing each other, it was cold comfort to get my wish … finally … and to discover that being a "child of divorce" isn't so easy as a young adult, despite how much I thought I wouldn't care anymore. Divorce is emotional for the children, regardless of their age, and it was incredibly emotional for me.

Hitting the Brakes:
Too Little, Too Late

Kendall had asked about her grandparents' divorce, which brought up complicated emotions for me. I did my best to explain it. "I distinctly remember getting the phone call during my junior year of college from my mom — she'd finally done it, packed up and moved out."

I continued, "It was the last semester of the year, my hardest course load yet, and finals week. It was a Wednesday afternoon in late April, and I was studying in my upstairs bedroom of the off-campus house I shared with five of my Pi Beta Phi sorority sisters. The house phone rang, and I picked it up."

My daughter looked at me quizzically.

I sighed. "Kendall, before cell phones, each home was assigned a phone number and people would call that number and ask to speak with someone specific who lived there. If you answered, and the call wasn't for you, you'd yell out someone else's name and say, 'It's for you!'"

"Seriously, Mom, I know what a home phone is."

Whatever.

"Anyway, recognizing my voice, my mom, sounding out of breath, blurted out, 'I'm divorcing your dad.' I somewhat didn't believe her because I'd heard it many, many times before. But then she explained all the details of what transpired the minute my dad pulled out of the driveway and drove to work. A few friends arrived to help her load up furniture and her belongings as fast as possible — in case someone drove by, saw what was going on, and alerted my dad. She found an apartment on the edge of town and had told no one where she was going. In shock, but more annoyed than invested in this news, I said I was happy for her newfound freedom, but I really needed to get back to studying. I was literally emotionless. After all, I purposely chose a college several hours away to escape the dramatic life they continued living long after Beth and I moved out, desperate to create a fresh start for ourselves. I had neither the time nor desire to become distracted by them."

I continued my story while Kendall sat cross-legged on the couch, with a throw-pillow in her lap. Beth was sitting in an armchair across the room, filing her nails and nodding as she listened and observed my best impersonation of Rocky in a tirade. I have always been quite an entertainer.

After my mom had called me at college to tell me she had left my dad, I went back to studying for my exams. A few hours later, the phone rang again. This time, it was my *very* pissed-off dad. I barely said "hello?" into the receiver before the screaming started.

"Do you know what your cunt mother did today?"

You knew he was at the highest level of pissed when he pulled out the nasty c-word! To be honest, I had no idea he even had my phone number!

He asked if I knew where she was, and I denied any knowledge of her move or her whereabouts; I truly *didn't* know at the time where she was moving. It was then he laid down the ultimatum. He bellowed through the phone, "You can't have it both ways. You need to make a choice; it's either you take my side or follow your bitch mother. Who's it gonna be?"

Disinterested in playing his games or giving him even an inch of control over my life anymore, I told him he can't force me to choose a parent because this is not my fight. He interpreted my refusal to comply with his demands as disobedience and rightfully assumed that meant I sided with my mother, so he hung up on me. That decision would result in almost a full year of estrangement between Rocky and me, which honestly was not much of a change or sacrifice anyway. The unexpected collateral damage of my parents' divorce were the deep wedges it caused between individuals and factions throughout our entire family. Beth became estranged from my mom due to her disagreement with many of the choices my mom had made just prior to and following her leaving my dad. My dad, ever the pot stirrer, somehow convinced Beth that I had stolen items of hers that were being stored at our childhood home (which I never did or would ever do) and because I chose to maintain a relationship with my mom, Beth essentially cut ties with me as well. And I didn't think our family could be any more dysfunctional! It was devastating, to say the least.

I set the cordless phone down and immediately screamed "Fuck my life! My parents suck!"

Why was it that my mom finally chose to leave when she was alone with him? Because *she* couldn't take it anymore? Why didn't she make that choice when *we* needed her to? I spent 18 years in that hell, and she was finally getting the strength to leave when it was too late to save me and Beth. It was too little, too late, as far as I was concerned.

Rebounding from turmoil and distraction the way I always have, I blocked them out of my mind, continued cramming for finals, and chose not to discuss my parents' divorce with any of my roommates or friends. That final semester of college resulted in a 4.0 GPA and would aid in my graduating with high honors the following year. If there's one thing I know for sure, it's that I adapt well and thrive during times of chaos and uncertainty.

Little did I know how much I would need this highly developed skill of resiliency later in life as a mother.

The shock value of my stories had seemingly all but worn off on Kendall. She was likely exhausted from a full day of traveling both in the car and on foot through my hometown. Her only comment in the wake of this late-night story was centered around my divorce from her biological father; she said she was grateful we didn't argue or make her life, split between two homes for many years, miserable or more difficult than it had to be.

Also feeling tired, both physically and emotionally, Beth and I decided to call it a night, too. We retreated to her bedroom, which is where I always slept when staying at her home, just as we did when we were little kids. It always brought me a sense of calm to be beside her, talking and laughing until one of us fell asleep, usually mid-conversation. And back when we were little, sleeping in Beth's childhood room on the eve of Easter or Christmas had its perks: it was closer to the presents!

As we lay there that night, me 45 years old and Beth 46, recounting the numerous ways in which we purposefully altered the trajectory of our lives in hopes that we wouldn't end up disappointing or ruining another generation, the subject of emotion came up.

"Were you sad when I called to tell you Dad passed away?" I asked my sister.

I knew we both had silently said our goodbyes— Beth having done so at his hospital bed years before and me a few months earlier when I was home for a book-signing as he was resigned to the couch with an oxygen tank and couldn't be bothered to acknowledge our visit. I was curious what she was thinking and how she was processing the fact that he could no longer subconsciously terrorize us or have an impact on our lives.

As I recall this watershed conversation, I can't possibly recount it verbatim, but I remember vividly her key comments and the spirit in which she delivered them. She said, "You know, Laurie, I've been sad about a lot of things where he was concerned. I've mourned the loss of childhood innocence. I've mourned the loss of our house. But what has brought me the greatest sadness is that he never really knew my kids — the grandkids who lived a mile away for their whole lives. He had so many chances at a do-over in life, which most people don't get. There are people we know who've lost a parent before they had kids or when their kids were too young to remember them, and they say, 'I wish my dad or mom had been able to know my kids.' What's sad is when we say that same sentence. Because *our* dad had been alive the whole time. He could have gone to Maddie's dance recitals to make up for missing ours. He could have seen William thrive on stage or watch any number of sports the kids did. I'm sad for him that he missed out on their lives, and because they really don't know him, I've told them both they don't need to fly home for the funeral. How can you be expected to grieve the loss of someone you've seen less than a dozen times in your entire life?"

I wanted to cry, listening to my big sister share her disappointment and pain. Beth continued, "I could psychoanalyze his choices beyond being an alcoholic. Initially, his excuse for refusing to come to holiday or birthday parties was 'Your mother will be there.' He could never set aside his anger about her leaving him, or he enjoyed the attention that being a martyr about her leaving him delivered. Or both. But going deeper than that, I've wondered if he just couldn't bring himself to see us as better parents than the ones we had — as better than *him*. Maybe that sting of reality would force him to acknowledge that, although he kept a roof over our heads and food on the table, he was a pretty shitty parent and husband most of the time. So, I guess that another part of my sadness is that I never got that acknowledgment or apology and now never will. And I swear to God, he'd better not haunt me as a ghost because I will lose my shit! That's all I need — to build a safe life for myself out of his grasp, move to Japan, and then be haunted in my middle age."

I laughed.

In some ways, my dad had always been a ghost, showing up in our lives only as a half-aware zombie and miraculously cheating death, repeatedly, in his own way of reminding us that "only the good die young." Maybe his death wasn't such a shock because we'd been primed for this, time and again. Our dad had been hospitalized three times within a span of roughly five years. The first hospitalization came in 2012, after he was drunk (surprise, surprise) and slipped and fell while walking into his apartment, breaking his hip. I didn't visit him after his accident but was told that the doctors literally "prescribed" a few beers prior to surgery so he wouldn't end up detoxing during or immediately after surgery and end up "coding" while they tried to repair his hip. I was with Josh at the Boston Marathon when I got the call about this incident.

The second hospitalization was two years later, in 2014, when my dad had a heart attack in the bar, fell off the barstool, and wasn't breathing for several minutes. He was placed in a medically induced coma, I think, due to swelling in his brain from the fall and they didn't expect him to wake up. A priest delivered Last Rites. Beth read him her grievances letter while he was comatose, and after five days, he woke miraculously and returned to life as normal, just days later. Nothing kept Rocky down for very long.

Having said her "goodbyes" and feeling ready to move forward, Beth didn't visit or speak with our father for most of the six years between our dad's second hospitalization and when he died in 2020, unless I'd come home to Marshall, and asked her to accompany me for a cameo appearance at the The Riverside.

Our father's third extended hospital stay was in 2016 or 2017, when he was admitted for renal failure and put on dialysis. He wasn't expected to come off dialysis or live, but in true Rocky fashion, he did both!

A few years later, I had an occasion to see my dad again. Kendall and I had gone to Marshall for a weekend in August 2020 — for my book signing after the release of my first book, *Welcome to My Life* — and before leaving town on Sunday, I told Beth that we should probably go see him and essentially say our goodbyes because we'd heard from his sisters that he wasn't well. We walked into his dirty apartment, which always smelled of stale cigarette smoke, even though he'd quit at some point and was hooked up to an oxygen tank, and he was laying on the threadbare couch. He seemed unsure of who Beth and I were, but oddly, he asked, "Is that Kendall?" It was scary seeing him like that — missing some teeth, the skinniest I've ever seen him — but it was really frightening for Kendall. We tried to make small talk with him for about five minutes and Beth said, "Did you see in *The Advisor* that Laurie wrote a book?" *The Advisor* was our local newspaper. He whispered out, "Yeah, your aunt gave me that paper, but I haven't read the article yet." No "I'm proud of you, kiddo" or "way to go," and he didn't even ask about how Skyler was doing. As we left (saying, "See ya, Rock" on our way out) and climbed back into Beth's car, I was the first to speak. I predicted, "I guarantee that is the last time we will see him alive." And I was right.

Now, here we were, in the dark together in Beth's bedroom, talking about the man who never expressed real emotion to us, never apologized to us, and never truly made us feel loved or seen or cherished.

"Let's face it," I said. "We weren't raised by parents who wore their emotions on their sleeves, nor were they forthcoming with what they were thinking."

I heard Beth take a deep breath and then sigh. "Well, I'm sure he came by it naturally, since Grandpa wasn't particularly emotionally available. Rocky was the apple of Grandma's eye; I'd dare say her favorite of the seven kids. He did have a source of unconditional love from her. I just wish she'd been more influential when we were kids, so we might have felt loved. You know, it's one thing for our aunts and uncles and grandparents and his bar friends to tell us often, 'Your dad sure loves you girls' or 'Your dad is sure proud of you girls' and understand now, as a parent myself that was obviously true, but it's quite another thing to be in my late 40s and not be able to recall a time I ever *felt* loved by my dad. Did I ever tell you what he said to me right before he walked me down the aisle at my wedding? He looked me right in the eyes and said in a slightly slurred voice (because, of course, he'd had a few beers prior to the evening ceremony), 'I really hate you.' I'm sure he thought he was being a little funny, playing 'the opposite game' or something, but not even being able to tell his daughter that he loved her on her wedding day reinforces how emotionally unavailable he was."

"And how infrequently we ever heard 'I love you' or 'I'm proud of you,'" I added into the dark. I was processing her story about my father saying "I really hate you" on her wedding day. I was too shocked to comment and gave her the silence she needed to continue.

Beth's voice was starting to sound more lyrical as she got more tired. We had long-since turned out the lights and crawled into bed. "I don't know. Maybe God will give him the chance to try life again and learn from his mistakes. Or maybe there are five people he'll meet in heaven whose lives intersected with his" — a nod to Mitch Albom's book, *The Five People You Meet in Heaven* — "and he'll learn the lessons he never did here on Earth. Maybe he will be able to understand and appreciate that I had to choose between being yet another one of his enablers and setting boundaries for myself and my children. I've carried a lot of guilt about that, feeling judged by all his bar friends and even our relatives, because I've been in Marshall through most of my adulthood. But dammit, Laurie, I didn't have a choice when I was a child to not deal with the bullshit that consumed every facet of our lives; I was not going to be on speed dial to come running every time Rocky fell off his barstool or couldn't manage to buy groceries for himself or clean his house or any number of things an adult should be able to do for himself. I'm not like him; *my* children were my priority, and I chose to draw my line in the sand 20 years ago."

"I certainly don't disagree with how you feel, Beth. I am a little shocked that he told you he hated you on your wedding day. I never knew that happened. I guess I should thank you, because seeing how wasted he was and how evil he became after your reception back at home, I swore on that very day that dad would never be invited to my future wedding. And he wasn't … for either of them," I joked. "The fact that he had zero interest in getting to know Skyler and Kendall pissed me off, and I used to blame myself — thinking that it was because I moved away, but I ultimately realized that it was a conscious choice he made, which had nothing to do with distance. I lost track of the number of times we've been told by people in town that Dad went to watch the bartender's daughter in her dance recital or that he purchased bikes, toys, engagement rings, and paid for college expenses to help random 'bar friends.' Never once has he sent a card to Skyler or Kendall, let alone bought them presents. So, I feel ya. Our kids were dealt a shitty hand when it came to our side of the family. I'm just grateful that all our kids have amazing relationships with our ex-husbands' parents."

"Mmmm …" Beth responded, drifting off to sleep.

"Well, I'm spent from this emotionally draining day, and we both know tomorrow's lunch date with Mom is likely to be just as exhausting," I yawned. "You know there is a silver lining to this crazy, shitshow of a family, right? God could've made you an only child. Goodnight, Bennie," I giggled.

A Fork in the Road:
From Abuse to Abandonment

Going home to bury my dad was a pivotal moment in my life. "My dad" — it's a phrase I have typed time and time again in this book, and a descriptor that has always felt a little wrong to me. Never in my recollection have I called my father "Daddy" — not even when I was a very little girl. And when addressing him, I didn't often call him "Dad" either. For the entirety of my life, my communications with my father were stiff and abrasive, defensive and — when I got older — offensive or distant, a way to protect myself and my children. I don't remember ever really "formally" addressing him, calling for his attention with "hey, Dad …" My communication with him happened as a matter of opportunity and need. If I had his attention, I would just speak — no "hey, Dad" or "but, Dad" or "Dad, I was wondering …" When he was drunk, Beth and I would talk to him like everyone else did, by saying "hey, Rock" or "listen, Rocky." Many adults who call their parents by their first names do it as a "stepping away" or a sign of a rift that happened over time. But for us, he was *always* Rocky. For us, we had never had a "daddy" at all.

Reflecting on how childhood trauma has influenced — my life and how it's shaped my role as a parent — has brought me to many epiphanies and a great deal of peace in recent years. But I have never been able to simply "move on" or to keep the pain contained simply to my relationship with my father. Toxic, dysfunctional families are a tangled web of pain.

Growing up in a chaotic, unhealthy, and emotionally void environment has significantly impacted all my adult relationships. It has shaped and flavored my relationships with parents, aunts, uncles, and cousins. It has impacted my interactions with colleagues and friends. It has played a role in both my marriages. And it has informed the kind of parent I have been to my children. I am a product of my upbringing, for better and for worse.

As an adult, I didn't really have a relationship with my dad; after I left for college, I was able to separate myself from him more and more. His death — and that late-night conversation with my sister after Kendall and I arrived in Marshall to plan the funeral — really served as the catalyst for this book.

The tougher pill to swallow — tougher than the realities of being estranged from my father when he died and tougher than the fact that he never achieved sobriety or became a good father or grandfather — has been the "dream deferred" of my adult relationship with my mother. I fully assumed that a deep bond with her would only grow and strengthen as we both aged and experienced together all the twists and turns adulthood threw at us. I'd always envisioned the two of us talking daily on the phone, her imparting words of wisdom and plentiful opinions masked as suggestions about my life choices, along with frequent smirks and mentions of "payback" when she notices her granddaughter acting "just like you did at her age." I expected all of this to make me roll my eyes while secretly savoring every moment because I knew deep down that it came from a loving, caring, and emotionally invested place.

Unfortunately, our journey as mother and adult daughter has not resembled that dream scenario. Instead, our sporadic, brief exchanges merely cover the same checklist of questions and topics, ultimately leaving us both feeling uncomfortable and completely disconnected. I have tried, and I think she has tried too, but we always seem to come up short in creating the kind of connection we both need and deserve.

Now that my own children have reached adulthood, it saddens me that, once again, I lack a road map on how to navigate motherhood in the capacity that they each need me. As I've overcome my father's poor choices and behavior, using it as fuel to not just parent differently but better than him, I've come to realize the bond shared between Kendall, Skyler, and me doesn't have to mirror my relationship with my mother either. I can choose to be different from them both. I can choose to end all the cycles of family dysfunction, here and now. And forever.

When Beth and I awoke the morning after our guided tour of town — showing Kendall some of our favorite childhood spots — there was a nervous tension in the air. I'm not sure if it was because all the unhealed wounds from my dysfunctional upbringing had their Band-Aids ripped off over the past 24 hours, or if I was anxious about the lunch coming up with my mom … or both. I also had a funeral to help plan, a eulogy to write, and a father to bury, though I was managing to avoid thinking about the obvious. I found myself distracted and a little short-tempered.

Kendall made her way to the kitchen and, unknowingly, I gave her the look. A slight smirk appeared on Kendall's face. "What is that look for?"

"You know how I knew you were awake, Kendall? Because it sounded like a damn herd of elephants stomping around in Maddie's room," I joked.

"Ugh!! You always say how much your dad tormented you about making 'normal' noise, right? Well, you're tormenting *me*, Mom! You *always* get mad at me for being loud, but I'm *not loud!*"

She raised her voice at me, while arguing that she's not loud. Oh, the irony. I wasn't amused.

"And … You just proved my point. And if you think I'm bad, you should have grown up in my childhood home. Kendall, our dad was neither patient nor tolerant of what he perceived to be loud noise — even our talking in his presence was considered irritating. We never felt free to move about our home as carefree children, laughing and playing, unless our dad was at work or the bar. On the rare occasion he came home after work (which we only knew when seeing his car in the garage as we pulled into the driveway), Nana would warn us to just go to our rooms and be extra quiet. We complied like good little soldiers because none of us wanted to be subjected to another night of his bitching. Believe me, the irony was not lost on me — the man who hated noise always chose to scream and yell in a loud tirade to get his point across. It also amazed me that someone who was rarely around would have the audacity to dictate so many noise ordinances and rules within a home, all seemingly for the selfish enjoyment of stoking fear and anxiety in me and Beth."

Basically, my dad was like a tyrant librarian. Rocky took great pleasure in punishing us for being "too loud" when doing basic movements around the house. A variety of uncontrollable things ticked him off: wind slamming an open door closed; a heavy, dining room chair sliding across the linoleum floor instead of being gently lifted and set back into place under the table; a spoon or fork clanging or scraping against a bowl or plate when eating; or one of the most absurd infractions, flushing a toilet when — God forbid — he was napping in the basement directly under the plumbing! Even if I wasn't the culprit, I heard, "LAURIE! Get your ass down here!" howled from the basement. When I promptly hustled my frightened ass to the basement, I was always questioned as to "what the fuck" I was doing to "sound like a goddamn herd of elephants up there." And he always wanted to know "who flushed the goddamn toilet?!" The punishment was swift and either mentally or physically painful. If he was feeling generous or lazy, I wouldn't get spanked, but instead I was literally "grounded" on the spot and forced to sit near him on the adjacent couch for several hours watching torturous, old-people television shows like *M*A*S*H*, *Gunsmoke*, *Hee Haw* (which wasn't the worst of the mix because it's where I first became fascinated with clogging), *Lawrence Welk* or *Andy Griffith Show* reruns, boring professional sports (bowling) or old Western movies. Mind you, there were no remote controls back then, so ordering me to walk over and physically turn the knob of the television to change the channel (to one of the three stations we could get "out in the country") made my grounding much more purposeful and entertaining for my dad.

I always wondered why my mom didn't stick up for us and tell her out-of-control husband that his punishments were ridiculous, but it's crystal clear to me now that she, too, was afraid of him. But it did hurt me that she never argued back on my behalf. Hell, sometimes she pandered to him, telling us to hurry up so we wouldn't make him angrier, acting like she was on his side and in agreement with his demands. Perhaps she was just glad she wasn't on the receiving end of his bitching, for once — glad to be in his good graces momentarily while he focused his vitriol on us girls. I suppose that's why, even as an adult, it bothers me when she doesn't consider my feelings, doesn't proactively show up when I need her, or doesn't just check in on how I'm doing. Her indifference now highlights for me her indifference then.

Clearly, my mom and I trigger each other. I know I still resent her for lots of decisions she's made regarding me and, more recently, my children. I've had lots of therapy and understand the importance of talking through things instead of acting like everything is "fine," so I still get frustrated when my mom shuts down if a topic is brought up that makes her uncomfortable. If something causes us to butt heads, she shuts down, walks away or changes the subject. In the end, nothing is ever resolved.

I had always expected my bond with my mom would strengthen as I became an adult, and she would be heavily involved — almost to the point of being overbearing — when it came to the special moments of my adult life, such as planning my wedding and me becoming a mother. Instead, I feel somewhat abandoned and resentful of her distance, both physical and emotional.

My wedding to my first husband is one event that I believe started our disconnect. After becoming engaged, I was excited to talk through every detail in lock step with her, specifically when it came to my wedding dress. I thought we would reenact all the trips we took together to Patty's Bridal Shop in Quincy, Michigan, during high school to buy our homecoming and prom dresses. Only this would be even better and more special.

I recall sifting through every issue of *Modern Bride* and *Bridal Guide* magazine available, with the hopes of identifying my perfect dress. And I found it in the pages of one of those magical, glossy magazines! Now, to find it in a store. Back then, lacking the benefit of the internet meant you had to turn to the trusty phone book to locate the nearest wedding dress shops within the Yellow Pages section of that newsprint book. After numerous phone calls, I found a boutique in Indianapolis that had a sample of the dress available to try on, so I could get a better idea of what it would look like on me. Beyond excited, I immediately called my mom and asked if we could pick a weekend to meet there. Remembering how much she enjoyed helping my sister select her wedding dress (also at Patty's Bridal Shop in Michigan) years earlier, I figured sharing this experience with me would be exactly like that. However, during our phone call, she said she wouldn't be able to meet me. I was crushed. Who wants to select their wedding dress alone? So, lacking any other options, since my fiancé and I had just moved to town and I didn't yet have any local friends, I asked my soon-to-be-husband to go with me. We agreed that he would wait in the car though, so he wouldn't see the dress and spoil the surprise reveal at our wedding. Back then, I believed in all the superstitions about "good luck" at a wedding, despite subconsciously ignoring obvious red flags in our relationship, but I digress...

The store was super busy with never ending rows of beautiful white fabrics covered in lace and ornate beading, so locating my specific dress seemed like finding a needle in a haystack. Immediately overwhelmed, I asked the first employee I saw for help. I handed over a photo of the dress, a torn-out page from *Modern Bride*, and she led me to the exact spot where the dress was hanging. While handing me the gown, she glanced at my 5'2, 125-pound frame and said, "Oh no, this sample is a size 12, which you're going to swim in. But don't worry, we have some clips you can use to cinch it tighter to give you a better idea of how the correct size will fit you."

I followed her to the large, curtained-off room where several future brides were also trying on armloads of dresses, and she kindly instructed me to let her know if I needed anything. I quickly glanced around the room, found an empty spot to hang the dress, and was suddenly overcome with heavy sadness. Here I was, surrounded by the cheerful smiles, laughter, and happy tears between mothers and daughters sharing this special moment together, and I felt literally and figuratively alone. I turned to face the corner wall, hoping to blend in, and did my best to pinch and gather the excessive fabric around my body, which was not working. Meanwhile, unbeknownst to me, one mother and daughter pair had been observing my struggle. They stopped their bonding time to come and help me. I fought back tears as the mother pulled my dress upright and her daughter applied the clips along the back. They both told me how lovely it looked on me and that I was a beautiful bride-to-be. In classic Laurie fashion, I repeatedly apologized for interrupting their experience and thanked them for the help before practically sprinting out of the store to my oblivious future husband, who was waiting in the car. It would be a few days before I called the bridal shop to order the dress.

I just wanted my mom. And I wanted her to be loving and invested in me, like everyone else's mom seemed to be. Was that asking too much?

Sure, my mom and I experienced what I would consider normal irritation and bickering between a mother and daughter, but that's not what left me reeling. I think I'm the saltiest over the fact that I have felt emotionally abandoned by the most important person in my life; growing up, it is said that a child's most important relationship is the one with their same-sex parent. And while she was there for us in all the ways she knew how to be when Beth and I were little, my mom essentially watched us leave the house to head off for college and seemingly thought we were "all good" to face the world without her. But we weren't. We still needed our mom.

Perhaps it's not fair to place expectations on our parents as to their level of involvement and attention toward their adult children and grand-children — attention toward us once we're in our 30s and 40s and beyond, and attention toward our young children who might benefit immensely from close relationships with their grandparents. However, when you grow up with a mother who volunteered to organize every school function, chaperoned field trips and semi-formal dances, sewed costumes, arranged fundraisers, and literally raised her hand to participate in anything that would temporarily remove her from our destructive household while simultaneously cementing the bond with her daughters that she seemed so desperately to want, it's difficult not to be disappointed when her excitement level around getting to know her grandchildren is surface level, at best. Her reasoning for that, when I was brave enough to ask, was not a response I expected: "I spent 25 years in hell married to your dad, and I raised you girls by myself. I've moved on, and it's my turn now to do what I want with my life. You should just be happy for me."

I had long since come to terms with the childhood I had endured, but I still had hopes and plans for today and tomorrow. Considering that my dad was incapable of forging a relationship with his own kids, I predicted a similar outcome when he became a grandfather. Like my sister, though, I often held out hope that he'd surprise me. After all, the role of grandparent presents an opportunity for a "do-over," a mulligan in the golf game of life, which, in my case, could redeem my lousy childhood and allow me to see some growth in his character and priorities. But he repeatedly made the conscious choice not to involve himself in the lives of his four grandkids, two of whom lived just a few miles away. Instead of accepting invitations to attend birthday parties and dance recitals, his preference was to spend Saturday afternoons perched in his favorite corner bar stool at The Riverside and allow history to repeat itself.

Granted, moving four hours away from my hometown was my choice, and I never had unrealistic expectations of either of my parents visiting monthly or, in my dad's case, visiting me at all (which in 22 years he never did, by the way). However, when my mom has traveled to Indiana, usually to attend one of Kendall's activities, since Skyler rarely participates in any, the focus has not appeared to be a chance to strengthen her relationship with her grandkids or getting to know them as individuals. Instead, her visits predominantly serve as an opportunity to show her Facebook followers that she's a doting Nana, and maybe to convince herself of the same.

I was used to this behavior from my dad. In high school, Beth and I worked several different jobs, which meant interacting with people in the community on a regular basis. I can recall hearing many times from customers who interacted with Rocky at the local taverns, "Your dad sure is proud of you girls." I'd smile and thank them, but beneath it all, I was pissed. First, how dare he brag about us since he infrequently watched us dance and never watched us play sports? I never felt he had a right to share our accomplishments because he chose not to be involved in our lives.

Second, why was it so easy for him to tell random patrons at the bar how proud he was, but never—ever—told us?

So, when my mom comments on or shares the accomplishments of her daughters or grandchildren on social media without sharing a true, authentic connection with any of us, it reminds me of my dad doing the same thing. It reignites that sense of fury within me, which she completely misunderstands.

When my sister and I dare to broach this subject with our mom, we are labeled ungrateful brats and reminded for the millionth time about the countless sacrifices she made on our behalf, while she suffered through that nightmarish marriage. Every time we tried to talk to her about the present and the future, she relitigates the past.

Had my mom been more emotionally available for real conversations about my feelings or tried to gain a better understanding of my daily life parenting through autism, maybe I would have a closer relationship with her today that goes far beyond just photographs taken for social media. Sure, I have photos on social media and in albums and scrapbooks too, but they are collections of true memories and meaningful moments. The difference between the scrapbooks Beth and I have created — with countless photos of our children — and the periodic Facebook photos my mom shows off to her friends is that Beth and I have prioritized and valued the experience and opportunity to connect with our kids in those special moments, rather than just "pose" them. It melts my heart as a mother when Kendall will randomly pull those family albums off the shelf and ask me to revisit those joyful times with her. That is the connection and open dialogue I wish my mom and I shared. It's the connection I wish my mom shared with my kids.

For all the times a conversation has been quickly shut down by my mom the moment I mention Rocky or ask a clarifying question about the first 18 years of my life, I think to myself, *"What if I were this dismissive of Kendall when she comes to me to vent about issues with her dad,* (my ex-husband)*?"* I can't imagine telling her to "get over it" and move on. On the contrary, some of those tearful, deeply emotional, and slightly uncomfortable conversations I've had with Kendall as a young adult have solidified the close mother-daughter relationship she deserves — the kind of relationship I'd hoped to have with my own mom. To my knowledge, Kendall has never once hesitated to approach me, regardless of the subject, and ask me questions or openly share her thoughts and opinions. I've made it a priority to provide her with a safe place to express herself and feel heard, accepted, and supported.

In this regard, I hope I have done her justice. In July 2021, Kendall was 16, coping with significant anxiety and depression, due to the reprehensible treatment she was enduring from her step-mom — treatment her biological father allowed, doing nothing to defend or protect her. So, Kendall told her dad she wanted to live only with me for a while, no longer spending entire weeks or even weekends with her dad, his wife, and their young daughter. None of us knew how long Kendall might choose to forego her visits with her dad, but we all agreed it was for the best. Throughout the next 10 months Kendall thrived and was visibly much happier. It was important to me and Josh that she felt safe and comfortable to be vulnerable and share her thoughts and feelings with us about this transition and about anything else that was on her mind. So, each weeknight we would sit down for dinner together after Skyler went to bed (his preferred routine is to be fed dinner by 5:00 p.m. and in his bed by 6:00 p.m.) and the discussion topics could be about anything except autism. That's laid the foundation for the even closer relationship we share today.

While my relationship with Skyler differs considerably from the one I share with Kendall, largely due to his inability to verbally express himself, if Skyler were to ask me questions about his life via spelling with his letter board, I would never dream of ignoring him or responding negatively. I can't even imagine thinking, let alone saying, something to Skyler like, "The past 20 years of my life have been hell because of your autism! I've sacrificed a lot to raise you, and now it's my turn."

In May of 2022, on the Monday following Mother's Day, Kendall learned from her paternal grandmother that her father, his wife, and their young daughter had sold their Indiana home and moved to Florida. Yes, he moved and didn't tell his daughter. My reaction was not what Kendall expected because I got upset. She clapped back, "I thought you'd be happy that he's gone." But as I explained to her, I wasn't sad for me — I was sad for *her* because although she may not feel it yet, this is something that will pop back up in her adult life, causing her true feelings about being abandoned by her father (and the same thing happening to her brother years earlier) to come out. I didn't want her to feel the way I have felt much of my adult life.

Thankfully, she has continued therapy even into college, so she has had outside support in addition to Josh and me. Since her father's move two years ago (as of the writing of this book), Kendall hasn't received so much as a text from him on her birthday or Christmas, nor did he attend her high school graduation or text her a "congratulations." My ex-husband's only indirect contact with Kendall has been by paying his third of her college tuition, which he is obligated to pay from a legal standpoint. Although I was successful in keeping my kids away from alcoholism, I wasn't as lucky preventing them from being abandoned by their father.

I deeply value sharing a closeness with both of my children, in whatever way that connection presents itself. But the sad irony is that only Kendall can clearly validate whether my tireless efforts to make them feel loved, appreciated, and valued were successful.

For the entirety of my motherhood journey, I have felt required to morph into two unique versions of myself, adapting and learning how to attend to the drastically different needs of my children. I have made every attempt to be fully present and engaged in the precise and unique ways Kendall and Skyler need me, so neither of them ever feels neglected. But we do the best we can with what we've learned and observed from our life experiences. And my parenting guidebook was missing several chapters.

Mothering a child with severe, non-verbal autism is physically, mentally, and emotionally exhausting, and although I'm not dealing directly with alcoholism anymore, the excess amounts of strength, resilience, and patience required daily when supporting Skyler often takes me back to my lonely, overwhelming childhood. In many ways, my role as Skyler's parent and lifelong caregiver mirrors my upbringing. As the child of an alcoholic, I unintentionally assumed the role of "parent" to and apologist for my dad. At the same time, I became a caregiver for my mom, doing my best to support her emotionally and help her manage her mental health in an era when no one was reading self-help books, much less seeking therapy or outside support.

One of the biggest "a-ha" moments upon reflection of my own motherhood journey is that while I've spent much of my life longing for an emotional connection with my mom, it's not been a priority for her to reciprocate. I don't think there's any malice in her approach, just a sort of survival-instinct selfishness and sometimes a learned helplessness and indifference. Perhaps losing her own mother at such a young age affected her emotional growth. She never had an adult relationship with her mother either. Whatever the cause, my mom has been unable or unwilling to connect on that level with her daughters and grandchildren. And it's been hard for me to let go of the wish that she could and would.

This distorted relationship with my mom has always weighed heavily on me. All I've ever wanted and needed is for my mom to acknowledge that Beth and I suffered living in that home, too. Instead, I feel like I'm still walking on eggshells, only this time it's not my dad throwing the eggs. Every time I'm around my mom, I feel myself reverting to my childhood role as her caregiver. I delicately tiptoe around her feelings and give her insensitive words a pass, while my trauma is never addressed. The hell *we* endured gravely impacted our adult lives as wives and mothers, and we've been forced to teach ourselves how to be vulnerable and emotionally available for our children, so they don't struggle like we have.

My mom only recently acknowledged my feelings and apologized for making the choice to remain married, thereby removing any chance we had for a happier childhood — one that wouldn't require significant therapy to recover from. While it's a great start and gives me hope, until she's willing to work through her own past traumas, we will likely maintain a surface-level relationship. It truly saddens me to think that when Beth and I were young and visiting our friends' homes, we were envious of the strong connection our friends had with their dads. Now that we are adults, we are envious of their current close-knit relationships with their moms. As a kid, I just wanted a "normal" family. As an adult, I still want the same thing.

That fall day in 2020, one day after completing the first leg of the road trip to my father's funeral, Beth and I found ourselves bracing for an uncomfortable confrontation with our mom. We had made plans to meet for lunch at Grand River Brewery, and as Beth, Kendall, and I walked the two short blocks to the restaurant, I was already feeling on edge. When we entered the restaurant, my mom was already seated at a high-top table (which struck me as funny because, being 4'11, she always preferred sitting where her feet were closer to touching the floor instead of dangling two feet above it) and she smiled as we approached. We were barely seated when the waitress delivered our water and asked to take our orders. Luckily, we already knew what we wanted: salads for Mom and me, while Beth and Kendall both opted for the chicken sandwich. Although I settled on water with my lunch, today would have been as good a time as any to order a stiff drink!

As the waitress stepped away, Mom made the first move to break the awkward silence by asking Kendall how school was going. Even though we've gone over this ad nauseum, her reply to Nana was, "It's fine." As soon as I heard that, I immediately slapped my forehead - in my mind! Admittedly, I was a bit standoffish and quiet throughout the meal, but it wasn't just me who felt uncomfortable. You could cut the tension with a knife. We passed the time with typical pleasantries and with Beth answering my mom's questions about what her kids were doing given the drastic changes Covid had forced on their lives—since Kendall refused to use her large vocabulary and elaborate on her answers to similar questions. My mom made no inquiries about Skyler or Josh. No mention was made about the real reason why Kendall and I were in town. A painfully long hour later, as the checks arrived at our table, I became visibly irritated. I realized then that she was not going to bring up the obvious elephant in the room, so, despite my preference of avoiding confrontation, I did. Looking directly at my mother, I blurted, "So, are you coming to the funeral tomorrow?"

The speed at which she snapped back a seemingly rehearsed response made it obvious that she had been intent on sitting tight-lipped until one of us asked.

"No. I decided that I don't really need to be there. I broke ties with him over 25 years ago and have had little to no contact with any of his family members in all those years. Not one of them ever reached out to me or even cared about all the hurtful times I endured through my marriage to him."

I couldn't believe what I was hearing. Immediately I thought, *"How can she sit here and make my dad's death about her? Doesn't she recognize that, once again, she's abandoning us when we need her support?"* Whether we had a close relationship with him or not, we'd just lost our dad. I expected her natural response might be to ask how we were holding up or how we were feeling and getting by as we prepared for the funeral? I naively thought that maybe she would ask us if we *wanted* her to come to the funeral — if we would prefer to go it alone, or if we wanted her there to support us. But we had no voice in her decision. Flabbergasted, I told her she was selfish and inconsiderate, and then I stormed out of the restaurant, leaving my dumbfounded sister and Kendall there to attempt to explain to her why I was upset. I instantly called Josh to vent as I angrily marched back to Beth's house on what was otherwise a lovely fall Michigan day. My heart was racing. I was so angry and so hurt and feeling so … abandoned.

I'd like to think I have some perspective here and that I can put myself in my mom's shoes from time to time. As such, I fully understood — even in that emotional moment — that attending a memorial for her abusive ex-husband was not among the top 10 in my mom's list of priorities. However, if there was ever a time to take the focus from herself and recognize that being there simply because her daughters needed and wanted her there, this was the moment. I had hit my breaking point with her and just couldn't overlook her selfishness any longer. I was conditioned to expect neglect from my dad, but certainly not from my mom.

So, my mom's decision to forego my dad's funeral, even though she'd informed my dad's family members several days earlier that she *would* be in attendance, was a trigger for me. Although I'm not proud that I let my inherited short fuse get the better of me, it presented yet another teachable moment in my relationship with Kendall.

I swiftly arrived back at Beth's house, where I let myself in. Even though trusting that the world is still a safe and considerate place is a thing of the past in most communities, my sister always left her doors unlocked when she was still around town, like many families did when we were kids. I plopped down on a barstool at her kitchen island while Josh's calming presence over FaceTime worked to lower my heart rate. About 10 minutes later, Beth and Kendall walked through the door and filled me in on the conversation that had ensued after I'd left. My sister tried to explain to my mom that after I asked the question, she launched into what felt like a prepared speech in which she'd made things all about herself just as she routinely does. Beth told her that was the reason I called her selfish. My mom retorted, "Why is she being such a bitch about this?" and left. Mortified at all the inappropriate behavior of the grown-ups, me included, I apologized to Kendall for storming out of the restaurant and for raising my voice at her Nana. My mom has yet to apologize to Kendall for calling her mother a bitch. Before letting me explain further the backstory that provoked my outburst, Kendall wrapped her arms around me and said, "It's okay, Mom. I understand why you're upset." My heart burst into a million tiny pieces. That hug and affirmation was more than just a loving gesture between a mother and daughter. It solidified for me that, despite my shortcomings with demonstrating emotion, I've raised a child full of empathy, compassion, and affection. My past is messy; her future is bright.

Tank on Empty:

My Struggles with Affection

An hour or so after lunch, I had finally moved past the emotionally disappointing visit with my mom (for the sake of my sanity) and was ready for the next event on our schedule. The time had come to venture to Jackson, Michigan for a meeting with my dad's sisters, his brother, and the local church deacon, a lifelong family friend, who was chosen to deliver the graveside funeral service. We were gathering to discuss the funeral specifics, like music and scripture readings and how it would all work with Covid restrictions. Driving I-94 to Jackson, Beth and I couldn't help but reminisce with Kendall about the dozens of times we'd traveled these familiar roads, always with our dad at the wheel, usually destined for my paternal grandparents' house.

"We'd barely be minutes into the drive before we'd find ourselves having choking fits and blood-shot eyes, which were a direct result of being hotboxed by Marlboros in a backseat engulfed by Rocky's second-hand smoke," I told Kendall, who could probably imagine it as she sat in the backseat of Beth's car at that very moment. "Despite our pleas for fresh air, Kendall, our dad refused to allow the windows to be lowered even an inch during this 45-minute car ride from hell. To add to my suffering, Aunt Beth would dictate the seam of the leather seat cushion as the line between her side of the car and mine. She would insist that I not cross the mostly invisible barrier, thanks to the smoke induced fog, or touch her for the entire ride. So, in typical annoying little-sister fashion, I would hold a finger in the air as close to her as possible without making contact and repeatedly whisper, 'I'm not touching you' until she cried out to my mom to make me stop. That's always been my role — serving as a distraction from uncomfortable or awkward situations with sarcasm, teasing, or humor, even if my teasing was sometimes (okay 90% of the time) at my sister's expense."

Beth chuckled sardonically and let me continue.

"The return ride home was even scarier because my dad always drank far too many beers at extended family gatherings and thought nothing of driving the four of us home at highway speeds while completely intoxicated. I remember Nana arguing with him to let *her* drive, but his response was always the same, 'No one is driving MY goddamn car but me!' So, without any additional intervention from my aunts, uncles, and grandparents, our Lincoln squealed out of the driveway with my dad at the wheel. To add to our torture," I turned around and glanced at Kendall, "my dad insisted on blasting the volume of his favorite 8-track cartridge, Oak Ridge Boys, and loudly sang the bass part of the 'Elvira' chorus. 'Giddy up, uh oom poppa, oom poppa, mow mow.' He thought he was hilarious — we were not amused, often clinging for safety to the new stuffed animal or doll we'd received from Santa or the Easter Bunny."

There was something truly healing and freeing about visiting all these old places and memories with my adolescent daughter and my wonderful adult sister — while being the *new*, somewhat healed me. Talking about those awful car rides during *this* peaceful and safe car ride felt like a full-circle moment. With every hour we spent together on this funeral-planning journey, I felt like I was rewinding my past and getting a second chance to see my family — and these towns — anew. We arrived at the home of my Uncle Dan, who was my dad's only brother and served as executor of his will. Although our family reunion was due to somber circumstances, it was nice to spend time with those who loved and perhaps best understood my ornery and complicated father. I had numerous questions about his passing from those closest to my dad and quickly regretted asking. Apparently, Rocky spent his final days disgruntled, ungrateful, and lashing out at anyone who tried to assist him, including his siblings. Even after death, hearing how bitterly he treated people who cared for him to his very end, was embarrassing and beyond disappointing.

To lighten the mood, a shoebox full of photos from Rocky's youth was passed around with funny stories accompanying each black-and-white image. The handsome, smirking teen staring back at me had the face of a stranger. One of my favorite stories was the time my 6- or 7-year-old dad was picking on a girl in his classroom so much that she took her scissors from her little pencil box and cut the bottom off his necktie. I'm sure he deserved it, but never to be disrespected, he countered and used his scissors to cut off one of her pigtails! I can't even imagine the wrath of my grandfather when he learned what my dad had done.

Uncle Dan shared with us the time when Rocky unintentionally broke his brother's nose. Dan was 6 and my dad was 11. Dan had just finished a bath and was trying to open the bathroom door to leave, and unbeknownst to him, my dad was holding the door closed from the outside. Uncle Dan kept tugging and tugging on the doorknob, pleading for my dad to let go while hearing giggles on the other side. One final pull from Uncle Dan at the same time my dad chose to let go sent the door flying directly into Uncle Dan's face, ultimately breaking his nose. It was confirmed that Rocky got a "royal ass whippin'" for that prank.

Beth, who is routinely more vocal than me when openly sharing the daily hell Rocky dished out, felt compelled to remind everyone in the room that we have very few fond memories of our dad that generate laughter when recollected. We openly vented about the significant absence of affection in our household and how that gravely impacted our comfort level with giving or receiving physical affection in our adult lives.

My childhood was not filled with hugs, kisses, and "I love yous" from either of my parents or an outpouring of compliments and encouraging words, particularly from my dad. But after digging deep — VERY deep — into my memory, I was able to salvage just two scenarios. In both instances, my dad shocked the hell out of me when he initiated a nice gesture, momentarily demonstrating that he at least liked me.

My first recollection of Rocky's ability to be kind was at age five. For months leading up to my 5th birthday, I had begged and pleaded for a kitten. I got a plethora of excuses from my parents as to why that would not be happening, most notably because they didn't believe I would take care of the kitten as I promised to do. As my Kermit the Frog and Miss Piggy-themed birthday party concluded and the adults remained in the garage smoking and drinking, I snatched up as many of my new toys and gifts as I could hold and took off in a sprint to my bedroom to put everything away. Not realizing my parents had followed behind me, I turned to find them standing at my bedroom door, my dad awkwardly shifting his legs left to right while his arms and hands hung low to the ground as if he was using his arms and legs to shield me from seeing something that was behind his calves. Unable to keep up this little hallway dance, he raised his arms high and gingerly side-stepped to reveal the tiniest little caramel-and-white-colored kitten pouncing around behind him. I squealed in excitement, "Is this kitty mine?!" Getting that kitten, who was lovingly named Butterscotch, was one of the best birthday gifts I ever received, and the fact that it was from my dad was as surprising as it was confusing. For my sister, it was an annoying nightmare — Butterscotch was all snuggles for me and all "achoo!" for Beth. Getting that kitten was how we learned Beth was allergic to cats.

Beth's allergy to Butterscotch did not prompt us to get rid of the kitten, though. It turned out that my dad really loved that cat. So, despite how illogical (and cruel) it might have been to keep a cat, knowing your child was allergic, that's exactly what my parents did. And despite my dad's constant screaming, which caused the cat to run and hide in fear, Rocky always claimed that "Butter" was "calming" to him. So, I think it's safe to say that my dad favored the cat's existence in our home over Beth's. No big surprise.

Getting my first kitty was a pure, sweet memory. The only other gifts I recall receiving from my dad were candy or trinkets he had picked up on his sales route — and they were almost always given to us following a huge, drunken blowup at home the evening before. Beth and I were ages 7 and 6, and I thought nothing of it; I was excited to get presents for seemingly no reason at all but, as I grew older and wiser, I recognized that these were intended as apology gifts that he assumed required no "sorrys" or explanations attached to them. They were bribes for our silence. It made me feel icky and confused that accepting his treats was insinuating forgiveness, so when I stopped acknowledging them as I grew older, he stopped "apologizing" completely.

The only other affectionate, bonding moment I recall sharing with my dad was during the frequent episodes of excruciating leg pain I experienced roughly from third grade through fifth grade. Looking back on it now, I would suspect that the pain in my shins and knees was due to the many hours spent at the dance studio leaping, tapping, and turning on a cement dance floor, but I now find it comical that my parents labeled this phenomenon as "growing pains" because I was always one of the shortest kids in my class and never seemed to grow. I would wake up in the wee hours of the morning, hollering in agony from my bed, and if I didn't get an immediate response, I often crawled to my parents' room, begging them to make the pain stop. Surprisingly, my dad would be the first to assist by grabbing his surefire remedy to fix me — Deep Heat. Now this wasn't your average Ben-Gay ointment; this concoction, housed in a large, dark-brown glass bottle with a sponge applicator, was hidden away in my dad's medicine cabinet, only coming out during my time of need. I think we had that same bottle for the 17 years I lived there. Like magic, after my dad applied the product up and down my shins, I felt instant relief. A warm, almost stinging sensation covered my legs while the intense smell of menthol helped me quickly return to sleep — or maybe it was the intense fumes that knocked me out. Perhaps my dad related to me more in this moment than any other because of the pain and suffering he endured being born with a club foot. Due to that birth defect, one of his legs was slightly shorter and one foot was a size smaller than the other, often causing discomfort when he wore unaltered shoes to offset the imbalance.

Whatever the reason for my dad's willingness to apply a treatment rub to my legs, it always worked. Seeing that infrequent, thoughtful side of my dad always left me puzzled. He was clearly capable of parenting with kindness, so why couldn't he behave like this all the time?

His siblings, of course, knew that Rocky was an alcoholic, but still appeared shocked to hear how neglectful — both physically and emotionally — their brother was to his family and apologized to Beth and me on his behalf. They said that, had they known this was going on, they would've confronted him or pushed my mom to get us out of there. Easier said than done I suppose, but I appreciated hearing it ... despite not fully believing it. I don't harbor any ill feelings toward my extended family for not rescuing us or supporting us, but it's easier to believe they chose to turn a blind eye to his behavior rather than to acknowledge it. After all, Rocky was the spitting image of my grandfather, and I don't blame them for not wanting to revisit their *own* childhood trauma or get involved. Maybe they felt that they couldn't stop the cycle of dysfunction that my dad was perpetuating, but that they could choose not to directly participate in it.

The conversation then turned to our eulogies. Out of respect for everyone attending who didn't know all aspects of my dad's personality, it was requested that we keep our content "light." Beth and I got a chuckle out of that request. Being that I'm not a fan of public shaming, I assured them that I would comply with their wishes, to the best of my ability. I considered Beth more of a wildcard. I wasn't sure whether she would want to filter herself or her feelings. And I wouldn't blame her if she didn't.

On the drive home from Uncle Dan's, the topic of affection was revisited — how little of it we received as children and how different my childhood was from what I wanted for my children. And Kendall asked the question that I hoped I would never get from her. "Mom, is that why you don't like hugging? Because Nana and your dad never did it?"

It took me a long time — and lots of therapy — to understand why I would cringe at the thought of a loving embrace, particularly when someone leaned in to greet me with a hug. To put it mildly, the act of physical touch is the most foreign of the "love languages" where I'm concerned. To this day, it becomes extremely uncomfortable when anyone attempts to hug me, which saddens me because although I've prioritized developing a physical connection with my children, it remains a difficult obstacle that I am slow to overcome with anyone else. I think it boils down to the level of safety I feel with a person that enables me to remove my boundaries rather than a total intolerance for physical contact.

"It's not that I don't like hugging, Kendall," I tried to explain. "I just don't like it to be forced upon me as an expectation. As you've witnessed firsthand, it's been quite a struggle for Aunt Beth and me to outwardly demonstrate affection, even to each other. However, we've come a *hell* of a long way. Even you laugh at the way your smart-ass aunt and I prefer to say goodbye — barely leaning into one another and lightly patting each other's back while repeating 'peace out' or 'see ya.' What can I say? It's our way of poking fun at our childhood dysfunction. And it's a habit. What really becomes awkward and off-putting is when your Nana, who we've already established rarely hugged us growing up, now demands a hug the moment she arrives and leaves our homes, thus obligating us to reciprocate or risk hurting her feelings. We've tried explaining why it makes us uncomfortable, but we're labeled disrespectful and rude for refusing."

I sat in silence for a few seconds, pondering it all. Then I shook my head and summed it up "Boundaries. Your Nana just doesn't understand them. My parents have always been too much and never enough."

Kendall gave me a weak smile, and Beth just kept driving and adding in her two cents when she felt it necessary. Although there has been a significantly lacking consistent, loving connection between my parents and me — throughout my life — I was bound and determined when I became a mother to ensure my children would always know and feel my love for them. I wanted them to feel it and see it and hear it through both my words and actions, no matter the circumstance. It was critically important for me to break the cycle of distance and dysfunction, so Skyler and Kendall never felt dismissed by me or struggled to establish a closeness with me or anyone else in their lives who mattered to them. So, from the moment they were born, I've showered them with an obnoxious amount of praise, encouragement, hugs, kisses, and "I love yous." Perhaps it has been as much for my own benefit as for theirs. They deserve loving parents, and I deserve an authentic familial connection in whatever way I can finally get it.

Affection, as it has turned out, is somewhat complicated for the family I have built — for me, Josh, Kendall, and Skyler. For the past 20 years of Skyler's life, I have spent practically every waking moment showering him with positive affirmations while also physically demonstrating how much I love and believe in him when assisting him with every task — dressing, eating, showering, communication, etc. Although deep down, I am quite certain that he appreciates everything I do for him, and I know that he truly loves me back, it sometimes saddens me that I've not yet heard him (and may never hear him) initiate or respond with "I love you, Mom." Knowing that Skyler generally avoids all forms of affectionate touches, such as a hug, snuggle, or kiss, I thought all hope was lost of ever receiving reassurance from Skyler of how he feels about me. However, one of the many reasons I'm so grateful to be married to an incredibly thoughtful partner is that he understands just how badly I need to feel connected to Skyler, since he's unable to verbally communicate his thoughts and feelings to me. So, for years, before Skyler went to bed or left the house on an adventure without me, Josh would say, "Skyler, give Mom a hug and a smooch." It used to fall flat, and the request was ignored. But I'm over the moon with excitement because within the last year, Skyler suddenly responded and now proactively leans into me to return those gestures by placing his hands on my shoulders (his hug) and quickly shares a peck on my cheek or forehead — wherever his unbalanced posture forces his kiss to land. It may seem like such a small thing, but to a mother who desperately needs confirmation that her child sees and feels how loved he is, I never take for granted a single reciprocated demonstration of affection, however it comes.

The open dialogue and close relationship I share with Kendall is without a doubt what I envisioned having with both of my children. Due to Skyler's profound need for support and nonstop attention, I made it a priority to carve out one-on-one time with Kendall. From reading books in her bed and impromptu dance parties in the living room to "Mom and Sis movie nights" and summer days spent doing arts and crafts or cooking/baking together, seeing the joy in her eyes while spending quality time alongside me has always warmed my heart and filled my love tank. Although our one-on-one quality time has decreased as she's aged (because hanging with Mom isn't as cool as it used to be, and because she's legitimately a pretty busy young woman), I value and never take for granted every meaningful conversation we share or her random requests to watch *House Hunters* together. Watching her grow into a thoughtful, energetic, respectful, confident, and affectionate young woman makes me extremely proud of her. And, extremely proud of myself too, for overcoming my own deficits to be the parent she needed and deserved.

We arrived back at Beth's and jumped into action, quickly whipping up some simple snacks because our childhood friends, Bob, Aimee, Gregg, and Beth J. were coming over soon. I try to get together with Aimee every time I'm in Marshall, but this visit was particularly important; her father-in-law, Ed, had recently passed away, and this was a chance for us to mutually share our respects. Bob, who I hadn't seen in years, arrived first and it was instant familiar banter, like no time had ever passed. He was my first and only serious boyfriend in high school, and we dated for the bulk of three years. Like Aimee, Bob was entrusted to hold tight to the chest the secrets of our family dysfunction. He always got along well with my dad and showed him respect even when I didn't feel he deserved it. My dad always said that he liked Bob from the first day he met him because Bob insisted on introducing himself and shaking my dad's hand before taking me on our first date. Bob was truly sad when he heard that Rocky died, having never apologized to me, Beth, or our mom, or making the effort to change. A few times over the years he saw my dad at The Riverside, and after exchanging pleasantries, it seemed that while most of the people from my past had moved on with their lives, my dad's life was stunted.

The last friend to arrive was Beth. We all used to dance together at Miss Bobbi's in middle school, and she and my sister were always close friends in school. Bob and the two Beths graduated in 1992, Aimee and I in 1993 and Gregg a couple years later, but being that there were many siblings a year apart like my sister and me, our combined classes represented one big friend group. We laughed and shared funny high school memories with Kendall, often interjecting bits of "how Rocky ruined that moment." I'm not sure if Kendall fully believed what I'd told her on the drive up about her mother being an innocent and respectful teenager, but after this small gathering turned into a tell-all, she likely hasn't a shred of doubt.

It was getting late, and I still needed to type up and print my sloppily handwritten eulogy, so we hugged and thanked our friends for helping to lighten the heaviness that filled our hearts the past few days. The funeral was at 10:00 a.m. the following morning, and I needed some sleep. After all, the day started out steeped in dysfunction from our lunch.

Tinted Windows:

Perspective and Perception

Saturday morning, October 10, 2020, was forecast to be a chilly and windy fall day, not ideal for an outdoor service, but the chill seemed on brand for the moment. Perhaps it was a subtle wink from my dad. The family had chosen to host a private graveside service at St. John's Catholic Cemetery (where all of our Sullivan relatives were laid to rest), and Rocky's urn of ashes would be buried alongside his mother's casket. I knew that Josh and Skyler were en route, having left our Indiana home a little before 5:00 a.m. to ensure they made the 10:00 a.m. service. Beth, Kendall, and I arrived at the same time as most of my dad's siblings. Outside of the extended Sullivan family, other attendees were Josh and Skyler (the only person, thanks to his adult stroller, who was seated comfortably); Beth's best friend and our dance sister, Kristin Ramos-Keyes; Courtney Crowley-Burk, our cousin from my mom's side; Feef and Rick Dillon, the couple I babysat for and considered to be bonus parents; and a few members of The Riverside bar staff. We were summoned to gather around the grave site by Deacon Mike McCormick, and I began feeling a small lump form in my throat. After several days of dredging up old baggage and once again finding myself at odds with my mom, delivering the eulogy I'd finally written became the least of my concerns.

Deacon Mike began by sharing a few funny anecdotes about my father to the handful of graveside mourners. My dad died during the COVID-19 pandemic, so small gatherings outdoors were all that was recommended; that's why we met at the cemetery and skipped a funeral-home "visitation" or church service or other indoor gathering. We didn't have much choice, and it was really for the best anyway. The entire time Deacon Mike was speaking, my eyes were fixed on the easel which held the large, framed 1966 high school senior-class picture of my dad (it was his absolute favorite photo of himself because, in his opinion, he looked like "the Fonz") and the urn adjacent to it that held my father's ashes. While staring at those objects, the finality of the moment hit me. This was truly The End.

Buried with him would be many unspoken topics and unanswered questions, never to be addressed. Buried with him would be long overdue apologies and explanations for why his internal demons controlled his life and ultimately ours. Buried with him would be the opportunity to get to know his grandchildren and possibly become a great-grandfather. To my surprise, I became visibly emotional, standing beside my sister as tears streamed down my cheeks. The once small lump in my throat turned golf-ball-sized while reading my eulogy, but looking directly into the eyes of my husband, son, and daughter — the beautiful family I've been blessed with — certainly helped me get through it.

Releasing all the inner turmoil I'd held onto throughout my lifetime proved a harder task than I'd anticipated; however, it was therapeutic to speak my truth and officially say goodbye to my father and the control he maintained over my life. These were my parting words:

> *Over the past few years, as my dad's health issues became more frequent, I often thought about this very moment and the many ups and downs our relationship has experienced. To be truthful, it was not exactly easy being Rocky Sullivan's daughter because he was not a man of many words — unless they were colorful swear words, so I never knew if he was proud of me or how he felt about anything, really.*
>
> *My dad was a lot of things: hard working, competitive, fiercely opinionated, funny, impatient, unemotional, loud, and hard to please. I inherited all those traits, the good and the bad, to some degree, along with his piercing blue eyes, and I couldn't be prouder. I have often caught myself saying the phrase "I can thank my dad for that ..." However, it's usually*

when I'm yelling or losing my patience with one of my kids or making someone laugh with my incredible gift of sarcasm and humor. Whether he intended for all those characteristics of his personality to be teachable moments and life lessons for me later in life, I'm not quite sure. What I do know is that I am resilient, independent, and meet challenges head on and with plenty of emotion, which I owe in large part to my dad.

Some of my favorite memories of my dad revolve around his talent for sales and love of gardening. I like to think my successful sales career developed by watching and learning from him interacting with his customers and him teaching me to sell vegetables. My dad wanted my sister and me to enjoy gardening as much as he did so he "let us" select and plant the various seeds in our garden. I thought the entire process was great until it came time to keep up with weeding and maintenance. Every weekend, Beth and I would hide out, hoping to get out of that horrible chore, but inevitably would hear the loud demand for us to promptly "report to the backyard!" After some whining and Beth claiming she couldn't help due to allergies, I — often alone — stood side-by-side with my dad as he proudly taught me everything he knew about proper gardening. To take the process full circle, he always set up a produce stand in our front yard for us to sell the veggies and learn how to make an honest dollar. We were allowed to keep the profits to buy school clothes or use as spending money at the county fair.

One of my dad's favorite tales to tell from my childhood was the day he took 8-year-old me to the bar to sell some corn. Quite the confident kid, I approached each intoxicated patron and almost sold-out minutes after I started — of course, I made sure to tell each customer how my dad made me pull weeds in the hot sun. My dad just shook his head, but I could see him beaming with pride at my smart strategy.

From then on, my dad labeled me with a new nickname, "Little Swindler."

That bar was where I spent many hours as a child. On most Saturday afternoons when, Dad would holler out "Who wants to go to the hardware store?" to which Beth and I would compete as to who responded first. We both knew that "hardware store" was code for the local watering hole, and the lucky kid who got to ride shotgun would not only get out of cleaning the house with my mom but was in for a full day, and likely night, of playing Pac-Man, drinking Faygo pop, and getting to wash glasses behind the bar. I truly treasured those moments with my dad because I felt important and enjoyed the rare one-on-one time it gave me with him. As I grew older and preferred spending Saturdays anywhere other than the bar, we grew further apart. He struggled being a "girl dad" and always proclaimed that he'd rather have sons. Thus, attending dance competitions over baseball tournaments was not his preference so he chose to be absent instead of uncomfortable.

Our relationship was tough and as a teenager, I missed the silliness and simplicity of being his comedic sidekick; his Punkin Pie as he liked to call me. As I stand here today, I am saddened by the many things I wish I had heard him say — that he was sorry for making drinking more of a priority than his family, that he was proud of me for all my accomplishments in life, and that he loved me. Deep down, I know he loved his daughters and was extremely proud of us but just could not bring himself to tell us those things instead of sharing it with random people at the bar. In recent years, I was able to sit down and have some lengthy discussions with my dad and found peace and forgiveness within myself for his temper and most of the childhood moments that were not so great. In the end, my sincere hope is that he was able to forgive himself for any unresolved feelings, unspoken apologies, or fractured relationships so he can truly rest in peace.

Although it was difficult to write a true reflection of the relationship my dad and I shared (or perhaps I should say "the relationship we lacked,") I'm proud of the words I chose. It was a tall task to provide a real and honest, yet thoughtfully crafted spin on some of the harsh realities of our life, rather than turning it into a roast of Rocky. But I believe I met the challenge.

Beth, who has always been introspective but doesn't shy away from speaking her mind, stepped up to read her eulogy. I was uncertain as to what angle she might have taken, mostly because we wrote them separately and decided to wait until the funeral to hear each other's words. I was holding my breath as she stepped up to the graveside with a piece of paper in her hands. It's mighty powerful that we both approached this with the same intention, and our stories slightly intersected, yet were unique to each of us. This is what Beth said:

If you'd asked me 30 years ago if I'd be standing here today giving a eulogy for my dad, I'd have probably rolled my eyes in the way only a teenage girl can and given you an emphatic "no." I didn't feel then like I'd want to mourn his death, and today I chose to wear blue — his favorite color — rather than black because I was right all those years ago. Well, sort of.

I am not really in mourning today because I have already grieved a lot of loss. Some of that was what I had lost, but most of it was mourning the loss of so many opportunities and life experiences for my dad. I understood how miserable and lonely he must've felt, especially the past 20 years, and mourned for him. And even though his alcoholism kept me from spending much time with him as an adult, it also gave me an unintended gift: the power of forgiveness.

That angry 16-year-old never imagined being able to forgive. And honestly, neither could the 26-year-old and 36-year-old versions of myself, either. But when he was on life #6 and in a coma, I wrote down all the things I never got the chance to say ... and I read them to him. I began to forgive all the hurt, mourn what he had lost, and open my heart to appreciation. This is why I'm wearing blue today. I'm not mourning Rocky's death; I'm celebrating that he is finally free of the physical and emotional pain that burdened him here on Earth. And I'd like to appreciate some of the more tender moments that were the only way he could express his love for us.

My dad was a hard worker who always made sure we had everything we needed and most of what we wanted. I never remember him taking a sick day, and my work ethic was directly shaped by him. He always talked about being the best paper boy in Jackson, and a lot of our Saturday mornings were spent on "business." I used to love it when he'd get out the cigar box that held all the loose change, so we could roll it and take it to the bank. When my fingers were too small to do it by myself, I just made the piles: 10 piles of 4 quarters, 5 piles of 10 dimes, 5 piles of 10 pennies. When we got a little older, we learned that the benefit of hard work in the garden would pay off in money for the fair and school clothes. Granted, we hated it and bitched and whined the whole time we had to pull weeds, but the dollars filling our money box — with all the heads facing the same way, mind you — helped us appreciate the work. Another glimpse into his character and business sense was teaching us to always throw in something extra. I learned what a baker's dozen was when I was 7 or 8, and we always bagged up 13 ears of corn for every dozen.

My dad was smart, though we didn't ever have intellectual conversations. I've always been a reader, but it wasn't until

I became a reading teacher that I reflected on his influence on that. He read the newspaper every day. He read the Reader's Digest *and gardening magazines and books about history. When he was home, if he wasn't watching the Tigers or* This Old House, *he was reading. And he was proud of learning Latin in school, so I think he appreciated that I also took Latin. But one of my favorite times was when he was doing a crossword puzzle and he let me help. He even had a crossword puzzle dictionary with a yellow cover that I wish I had today. The pages had discolored, and it had that old-book smell. And I loved it. I spent hours reading it and learning synonyms and antonyms and common answers. Today, I love doing a crossword puzzle with a perfectly sharpened pencil because "only a goddamn idiot would do them with a pen." {Sorry, Deacon Mike.)*

Even though he grumbled and was grumpy a lot of the time, I know some of it was just an act. He was sweet to us, too. Every Valentine's Day, really through high school, he brought home a box of those heart candies with the phrases printed on them. He was the only other person I knew who also liked black jellybeans, so we shared everyone else's. Even though a couple years ago he called Laurie to wish her a happy birthday on MY birthday, I know he knew our birthdays because he always played the lottery with our numbers: 3-1-7-4 was usually his 4-digit box number and 8-2-3 was his 3-digit.

We didn't really play sports in school, but we were very involved in dance. Even though he didn't love sitting there watching other people's kids, I know he enjoyed watching us — especially clogging — even though he couldn't stand listening to the noise when we practiced in the basement. He also always loved watching my best friend, Kristin, dance, and I know he appreciates having her here today and would be asking her if she still picks everything off her pizza like he did every time she came over since we were 8. In recent years, he may have sung karaoke down at The Riverside, but his most legendary performances was "King Tut" with the other fathers in a dance recital. Despite one (or four) pre-recital PBR's to knock off the stage fright, he did remember the choreography because he didn't want to let Miss Bobbi down. She and Grandma may have been the only two people who told him what to do, and he did it.

It should be comforting to all of us to know that he's in heaven, walking around on two feet the same size, where he's able to care for all of us in a way he wasn't able to when he was here.

As I stood by my father's grave, I couldn't help but reflect on the winding path that brought me here. I knew, in that moment, that my eulogy had been a powerful start toward expressing all that was within me, and my conversations with my family had taken me a long way toward acceptance and clarity ... but that I had work to do on my own heart as I continued to grieve and heal and move forward. The funeral marked the end of my father's life and the beginning of my ability to turn my pain into purpose. This book was bubbling forth before I even left the cemetery.

New Lease:

Life After Death

The drive back to Indiana with Kendall was much quieter. A lot had transpired over the previous three days but, in many ways, I felt lighter. For the first time in my life, I felt at peace. I set out on this road trip of memories with my daughter for the sole purpose and seemingly simple task of burying my dad. However, what I unexpectedly gained was an appreciation for myself as a mother and the confidence to commend myself on a job well done.

The warm embrace I received from Kendall, after tearfully and officially sharing a final goodbye to my dad and his hold over me, solidified that I'd broken the cycle. My children are comfortable with affection and not afraid of it. Hours and hours of enlightening conversations with my daughter confirmed that she wants to understand and connect with me, emphasizing that the bond I'd hoped to build with her is stronger than ever. In fact, the biggest revelation to come from this journey was that being Skyler and Kendall's mother has provided me the opportunity to write a new life story, one with a much happier ending.

Weeks after returning home, I was consumed with wanting to make sense of my life experiences and revisited the "Why Me?" discussion I'd had numerous times with God. Only this time, I actively listened and heard His words distinctly. "For I know the plans I have for you. Plans to prosper you and not to harm you, plans to give you hope and a future." Jeremiah 29:11.

Never had I put much stock in the concept that there is an explanation for everything beyond fate. But as I've grown older, and hopefully wiser, I no longer see situations or outcomes as coincidences, and I strongly believe that each of us has a predetermined plan for our life. Every closed door or bump in the road was intentional and meant to guide us one step closer to the bigger picture. There are no accidents.

It is through dissecting the past that I have discovered quite a bit about what makes me so strong and perhaps why God put every challenging and rewarding moment in my path in the exact order I needed to receive them. While wading through the childhood trauma, I uncovered that the little girl who was seemingly swallowed up by pain and fear was developing the skills necessary to be a fighter. If she was going to advocate on behalf of her children and herself, this was imperative — all according to His plan and timing.

It appears we learn our most valuable life lessons through our hardships and traumas. While these blips of time leave us with permanent scars, we often emerge with more enlightened perspectives on life. Regardless of the burden I carried throughout childhood, adolescence, and even adulthood, I know that being an alcoholic's daughter was and is not easy, but I learned universal lessons along the way. Despite all the uniqueness and independence within my sister and me, we are bonded by one thing: we had a drunk, belligerent, absentee dad we never truly knew or understood and who never really knew or understood us, either.

As a final step toward a profound internal cleansing, I was advised, once again, by my phenomenal therapist to write a letter to my younger self. Choosing to free myself from carrying those heavy burdens, resentments, and fears allows the little girl inside to finally heal and move on, too — Little Laurie Sullivan and Laurie L. Hellmann, we are a package deal. If I didn't release us both, the inherited impatience and anger wins and keeps me from embracing the beautiful blessings in my adult life — a loving husband and two incredible children.

So, in 2021, almost one year to the day of my father's funeral, I sat down to write this letter, which seems a fitting way to end this book. It took me a grand total of three hours and a whole box of Kleenex over a span of two weeks to write. I kept staring at the blank page, afraid to be vulnerable, and would grant myself permission to come back another day and try again. It is for me and her and you, and every child whose parents came up short, but whose potential was so much greater than the family dysfunction it eventually eclipsed. Our present is informed by our past, and our future awaits only after we have named those who have abused, neglected, and traumatized us, acknowledging how they had impacted us, and where we go next or how we grow from there. As I close this book, and literally close more than four decades of my life, "where I go from here" is a phrase that gives me peace and a concept that makes me excited and devoted and proud. Selling vegetables to drunks made me who I am today … and it taught me the value of resilience, empathy, and the unwavering human spirit.

Dear Laurie,

First and foremost, I want you to understand — and truly believe me when I tell you — that nothing you experience or have already experienced within your household is your fault. You should never be put in those situations, called those degrading names, or serve as your mother's emotional caregiver and support system. You do not deserve all that heaviness to be placed on your tiny shoulders. But please trust in my gift of hindsight that those challenges and burdens will provide valuable tools you'll need throughout your life.

There will be many difficult moments throughout adulthood that I want to prepare you for — broken hearts, failed relationships, unexpected parenting challenges you will encounter, and the infinite amounts of self-doubt and insecurities you will inflict upon yourself. But within the struggle, you'll find the significance and benefit that waits for you on the other side. Adulting takes quite a bit of adjustment, considering all the childhood baggage you bring into it. But I promise you, the joy and strength buried deep inside you is itching to reach the surface. Forcing yourself to let go of those deeply embedded negative labels and beliefs — the ones you repeat on a loop, day in and day out — will help you see the beauty within you and the world around you.

I must alert you that the word "autism" will quickly become part of your everyday vocabulary a few years following the birth of your first child, Skyler. However, that label doesn't define your son, nor will you allow others to use it to dictate his capabilities or underestimate his value. The constant advocating. The worry. The fear. The joy. The love. It's all-consuming, but completely worth it when you see how many lives are touched simply by your son's infectious smile and delightful giggle. You'll remind him every day that it's his superpower.

Rid yourself of the pressure to follow parenting books, forced timelines for achieving milestones, and "expert" advice on child raising. YOU, Laurie, will become the expert on Skyler and will quickly learn that he is the best tour guide through autism that you could ever need. In fact, you will author your own book detailing the challenging and enlightening journey you've traveled through autism, host a podcast (it's like a radio show!), and become a keynote speaker — all centered around that topic. Your honest and uplifting perspectives will be appreciated across the globe and serve as a guide for other parents and caregivers. Your title of "mother" will evolve as Skyler ages into adulthood, and you will embrace the responsibilities associated with being his lifelong caregiver and guardian.

Two years after Skyler's arrival, your beautiful, highly intelligent, talented, and quick-witted daughter, Kendall, will enter the scene. Unlike her brother, Kendall will demand complete independence from the moment she takes her first steps and insists on exerting control in every situation. Essentially, she is an exact replica of you, including the sarcasm.

Kendall will never keep you up at night — she won't leave you worrying whether she is making good choices, and she won't argue with you about doing her homework. She will discover her passion for dance, a profound love of reading like your sister (her book collection, although highly organized, will overtake the shelving capacity in her bedroom and annoy you for making the room look cluttered), and develop a close bond with her beloved cat, Snowflake, like you have now with Butterscotch.

Although Kendall doesn't ever complain or speak about the challenging and often confusing relationship she shares with her non-verbal brother or the many sacrifices she will be forced to make because of autism, just know that she internalizes her feelings and will need encouragement to confide in you. She has a huge heart and demonstrates kindness and maturity far beyond her age.

Learning how to parent two children who need you in completely different ways will be challenging. Oftentimes you will feel like you are failing them both (you aren't!) and will want to just give up (but you won't!). In their own unique way, Skyler and Kendall recognize your exhaustive efforts to teach them, learn from them, and most importantly give them a childhood they don't have to recover from.

Despite your first marriage ending in divorce (that's okay — it happens to a lot of people), you will demonstrate incredible resilience and courage as a single mother. You are capable of handling far more than you think, and your confidence is both inspiring and contagious. However, you won't be alone forever. God will place the perfect partner on your path at the exact moment He knows your heart is open to receiving him. Your second husband, Josh, is truly heaven sent. Josh will be the missing piece to your family puzzle. He is naturally supportive, hilarious, affectionate, confident, and spiritual and will inspire those same traits inside of you to surface.

More than anything, I hope by giving you a glimpse into your future, you recognize that life is truly what you make it. Don't let the power of the past overshadow the joy found in your present and future. The past merely provides a roadmap to who you are meant to become and for YOU, Laurie, the possibilities are endless. You hold the steering wheel, and the journey ahead is yours to navigate.

Motherhood will be the hardest and most rewarding job you were meant to have. And, spoiler alert, you absolutely crush it. Parenting Skyler and Kendall will provide you with the greatest gift — an opportunity to rewrite your story with a shift in perspective. It will allow you to experience childhood through Skyler and Kendall's vantage points. In doing so, you'll learn some valuable life lessons about patience, control, resilience, self-love, acceptance, vulnerability, and affection, which changes your outlook for the better. I promise.

Life will never be perfect, and you'll always be a work in progress, but you are more than okay. You are thriving and surrounded by people who love, admire, appreciate, and respect you exactly as you are. So, keep going.

Love,
Laurie

Epilogue

A lot of life has happened in the past four years since burying my dad. My daughter, Kendall, graduated Summa Cum Laude from high school and completed additional coursework at Ivy Tech Community College to also earn her associate's degree in the process. After spending what seemed like the fastest summer ever with her, I was caught off guard when the time came for Kendall to leave the nest and pursue her future dream career in veterinary medicine by attending Purdue University. Move-in day at the dorm gave me all the feelings. I must admit that stepping aside to let her organize and arrange the two SUVs worth of "college necessities" we unloaded was hard for this controlling mom. But as I said, I'm a continual work in progress, and I know she appreciated my restraint. It was my job to step back and watch her soar now.

After a lifetime of drop-off lanes and packing her backpack for school, getting her ready for a new academic year was suddenly (and profoundly) different. We were no longer going to "get ready for school" together each morning. She was about to be "on her own." Walking around campus brought back so many wonderful memories from my college days and I was so excited and hopeful that her experience would be just as fantastic. As the time approached to say our goodbyes, despite my promise to her that I wouldn't cry and cause a scene, I couldn't hold back my emotions. The tears that flowed down my cheeks were prompted by an equal mix of sadness, worry, and pride. I was sad to be losing the daily, in-person chats with my buddy. I worried about her safety when navigating the big bad world without my hovering and guidance. But mostly, I was proud to have raised a daughter with the confidence and dedication to venture into the next phase of life, making her own decisions.

I was also transported back to my college move-in weekend. In true form, my dad was absent from that milestone moment. I had navigated submitting college applications and scholarship essays, securing loans, and determining my major of study without any guidance or input from my parents, so when the time came in August of 1993 to pack up my things and go, all I really needed was a ride. My mom, along with my neighbor and childhood playmate, Kim, drove me the three hours to Ball State University to help me settle into my new home, a sixth-floor dorm within Lafollette Complex. Just as I had cried leaving Kendall, I recall my mom sobbing uncontrollably and not wanting to leave when she dropped me off at college. Poor Kim was a captive audience during the lengthy drive back to Marshall, as my mom expressed her fears and sadness of living completely alone in a house with Rocky. I think, deep down, the real root of her tears was knowing that attending college out of state was my long-overdue great escape from my dad's antics and torment, and it was highly probable that I would never be coming back.

Thankfully, this is not something I worry about with Kendall. She's not running away from our family in search of a better life, one not encased in dysfunction. Instead, she has been pushed and encouraged by Josh and me to run toward her dreams.

Typical of our divide-and-conquer lifestyle, Josh and I drove separately to Purdue because Skyler needed to be picked up from his autism center later that afternoon and, per usual, we had no one to step in and help us out. We decided to leave the decision up to Kendall about whether Skyler came with us to campus because, after all, we felt this moment should be all about her without her brother's autism taking center stage. Josh and I honored her preference that Skyler visit campus another time. In true amazing husband form, Josh instantly volunteered to hustle back home for Skyler because he knew how important it was for me to savor this once-in-a-lifetime experience with Kendall.

Kendall and I have taken many "road trips" together — to and from K-12 school, to dance competitions, on vacations, and on that fateful long drive to eulogize and bury my father (and my previously unsettled feelings about him). This time, I'd be making the return trip alone, leaving her behind and setting her free. This was all so new to me — so beautiful and profound and scary.

I spent my two-and-a-half-hour drive home thinking about my (now) adult children and how this was yet another significant rite of passage that only one of them will have the opportunity to experience. I was suddenly struck with a vision of the "new normal" of our household — new routines and dynamics without Kendall's daily presence. Instead of being empty nesters, Josh, Skyler, and I would forever be an inseparable party of three. Our weekends are spent in perpetual motion, trying to keep Skyler entertained, and our weekdays aren't any lighter. When Skyler (and all those with autism) turns 22 years old, participation in traditional programs and resources covered by state Medicaid services will cease. So, I spend hours each day consumed with often-fruitless searches for community programs and additional support that will provide Skyler with purpose and fulfillment. He deserves an opportunity to develop some independence. Josh and I would love nothing more than to see him excited about his future, just as Kendall is about hers. Driving home from Purdue, my thoughts bounced from Kendall to Skyler, and back again. I was a mom with a new set of expectations, and ongoing needs and challenges. I wondered, *What's next for us as a family? What's next for me?*

From those deep thoughts came the calmer, more optimistic, internal whisper that has evolved into a louder and more profound guiding voice that I'm learning to appreciate and follow. I was reminded to trust that everything will be okay no matter what circumstances come my way. I shouldn't try to micromanage the universe. By letting go of control, I'm opening the door to endless possibilities — those that aren't visible when I attach myself to the one "right" path. I have driven many roads — literal and metaphor — in my life, and I knew I could navigate these new roads, too. Upon arriving home, my fear and sadness about embracing change and the unknown was replaced with anticipation and an open mind for what is yet to come for our family.

We were doing well at home and Kendall was doing well at school; before life threw us another curveball. Things had been humming along with our daily routines, and I was finally able to sort through my feelings and emotions to put the finishing touches on this book — something I couldn't properly do until some time had passed after my dad's death. And then I received the devastating news from my cousin, Courtney, that her dad and my uncle, Gary, had been diagnosed with Amyotrophic Lateral Sclerosis (ALS) in late 2023, and it was progressing quickly.

Beth and I spent a lot of time with their family growing up. Aunt Sandy (my mom's younger sister) and Uncle Gary were chosen as Beth's godparents, and they have fully supported and encouraged both of us our entire lives. My fondest childhood memories of Uncle Gary are his "dad" jokes (which were very funny to little kids) and his singing, because he sounded like Elvis. He was always singing either nursery rhymes or popular songs from the '70s and would often dance with us, letting us stand on his feet as he swayed us back and forth. I couldn't help but smile when I was around him.

Uncle Gary was a bit of a local legend. On the St. Johns High School (Jackson, MI) and Hillsdale College basketball teams, he was an all-star guard. And he was well-loved by everyone he encountered. He also spent four years coaching Courtney's elementary school basketball team (although he continued "unofficially" coaching her in the driveway and her entire career through high school), coaching thousands of middle school kids, and was overjoyed to later mentor and coach his two grandsons, Courtney's boys Lucas and Harrison.

ALS is cruel. It affects the nerve cells in the brain and spinal cord, eventually causing loss of all muscle control. For an extremely active and energetic man who loved to dribble, shoot, laugh, and sing, being confined to a hospital bed in his living room and requiring assistance from others to move was brutal and heart-wrenching for him to endure. It was nearly as brutal for those of us who loved him to witness.

Only five months after his ALS diagnosis, my beloved Uncle Gary passed away on April 28, 2024. Shortly thereafter, I once again found myself headed to Michigan for a funeral. Only this time, I was overcome with sadness at the untimely, unfair departure of someone I loved and admired. With Kendall away at college and Josh hanging back at home due to Skyler's inability to manage a weekend hotel stay, this next road trip of mine would be taken solo.

Attending Uncle Gary's funeral, almost four years after my dad's death, was an intensely emotional experience for me. It brought back a flood of memories and feelings I thought I had buried with my father. As I sat among the hundreds of mourners filling the antique Catholic church pews to capacity, listening to my cousin Courtney's beautiful eulogy, I couldn't help but reflect on my relationship (or lack thereof) with my dad. Uncle Gary and Courtney had always shared a tight father/daughter bond; frankly it's one that I'd always admired and envied. So, it came as no surprise that in the weeks and months leading up to Uncle Gary's passing, Courtney was by his side, assisting with his care and savoring every word spoken before ALS would rob him of his voice. Courtney revealed to me that in his final days, she was able to have some important, private conversations with her dad, including sharing her eulogy with him, which he approved of. As she came to the end of her eloquently written tribute, not a dry eye in the church to be found, she concluded with the final words spoken between her and her father. In discussing how lost she and her sons would be without seeing and being around him each day, she asked him, "Where can I find you?" His reply, "You can find me in smiles."

My entire life, I had understood how vastly different my relationship with Rocky was compared to other friends and family who had an invested and involved dad in their lives. So, hearing about Courtney's last moments with her father set off a plethora of "what ifs" in my head. What if Rocky had chosen to reveal the true source of his anger and apologize to his daughters many years ago? What if I had been by his bedside, having long overdue conversations that would have allowed the closure and forgiveness we both desperately needed? What if he had made the decision to stop drinking and instead chosen to spend his remaining days and years supporting and loving his grandchildren? (Perhaps, then, they would have had a reason to mourn their beloved "Papa" instead of referring to him as "your dad.") What if all those times I was a captive passenger in his powder blue Lincoln Continental we could've had candid discussions about his childhood, so I may have understood him better? Perhaps I would have learned more about the "demons" Deacon Mike referenced at his funeral — the implied and never-spoken-about traumas that my dad was never able to overcome.

What if?

Following the funeral mass and reception for my beloved Uncle Gary, my Aunt Sandy invited everyone to gather at Key Largo Lounge (Uncle Gary's and her favorite local bar) to toast his life one last time. There was lots of laughter and sharing of funny anecdotes among the large crowd. It was touching for me to hear and see how many lives he positively impacted in his 78 years. A few hours later, as I said my goodbyes, Aunt Sandy introduced me to the handful of people she was talking to as, "my niece, Laurie, Judy's daughter." We spoke for a few minutes, and I learned they went to high school with Uncle Gary (where my dad also attended during the same timeframe), but I don't think they made that connection. So, I asked, "Do you know Rocky Sullivan? He was my dad."

All of them practically shouted in unison, "Rocky was your dad? Of course, we knew Rocky — everyone LOVED him, especially the girls!"

They asked how and when he died and continued on about the wonderful guy they remembered him to be.

This is what I've always found baffling. How could my dad be perceived as a funny, kind, and levelheaded man by his former classmates and bar "friends," but his immediate family rarely ever saw those traits in him? Had he changed that much since adolescence? Was he a chameleon who showed different colors to different people? Did something about marriage and fatherhood "trigger" him such that he felt he had no place to turn except alcohol and anger to survive it? To survive us?

The Sunday morning after Uncle Gary's funeral, as I loaded my car and prepared for a quiet five-hour journey back to Indiana, I was overcome with the desire to learn more about my dad's life before marriage and before my sister and me. I spent my drive questioning so many things. Aside from possibly *inheriting* my grandfather's love of alcohol and nicotine and adopting his fiery temper, why didn't he *choose* to break the cycle of addiction and abuse, as Beth and I had? I wondered if he once *was* a good person — a sweet and funny boy and young man. I wondered what it would have been like to know him like that. When did the switch get flipped where he seemingly gave up caring about hurting others and, ultimately, hurting himself? For all the negative things I can say about my father, I won't ever say that I thought he was happy at our expense. In truth, he was more miserable than we were. He was, perhaps, compelled to act out through addiction and violence. I don't think any of it made him happier or more fulfilled. I think it helped empty him and numb him and distract him from whatever he was running from his entire life (or at least his life from 13 onward, when his alcohol and nicotine additions began).

Those who knew Rocky's childhood best were his siblings, who lived much of it right alongside him, so my only hope in learning more about my dad was asking them to fill in the details and gaps in his life story. I hoped it wouldn't cause them harm by dredging up the past, but I was determined to learn more. In the coming weeks and months, I started reaching out to my aunts and uncle, asking questions I hoped they would answer honestly and in depth. I learned a lot. And I had my heart broken a little bit more. But this time for the boy my dad had been. In the end, I found additional healing.

One of the stories I had only heard bits and pieces of— until I asked — was that Rocky was born with a club foot. What I didn't know was that he had endured 12 surgeries and was in and out of casts for the first six years of his life. His older siblings recall pulling 5-year-old Rocky in a wagon as they walked to school. The surgeon made my dad and grandparents promise that he would never play sports beyond 8th grade because the intense level of athleticism required in high school could cause irreparable damage to his foot. So, when my dad was fully recovered, he was permitted to play both football and baseball ... but only through middle school. Knowing how much my dad loved baseball, I imagine watching his triplet sisters, Margie and Mary, play softball and his younger brother,

Dan, excel at baseball and be drafted out of high school into a minor league team was an incredibly hard pill to swallow.

If there is one comment made repeatedly about my dad, it's that he was sweet, adorable, and polite up through age 10 or 11. After that time, he developed an edge about him, rooted in sarcasm and defiance. He began drinking excessively around age 13 and some siblings note that his cigarette smoking started then too. I asked my aunts and uncle the obvious question, "What could have caused this major shift in him?" It was clear to me that he found alcohol to be the only suitable or available antidote for whatever pain he was experiencing.

I had always wanted to ask my dad, "Who hurt you?" And it was only after his death that I got the answer. He was the victim of sexual abuse by a trusted and powerful member of the community. I will leave it at that, not offering additional details, because, in the end, it was his story to tell (or not tell) and it's not fair of me to share something he chose to take to the grave with him. Something that drove him into the grave. Something that irreparably changed him and prevented him from being the adult he could have and should have become. Learning that a community leader was a child sexual predator — and that my father was one of his victims — made me sick. The fact that my dad, an innocent little boy, was robbed of a normal, safe childhood — and instead suffered in silence for the entirety of his life — is heartbreaking. It's not an excuse for how he treated me, Beth, and our mom. But it *is* an explanation. It should strike us as no surprise that he started drinking to escape the internal torment — to run away from the memories and the complex feelings of shame, fear, terror, anger, or even guilt. PTSD is a horror and substances, I would imagine, help keep the horror at bay. The abuse he suffered also is not an adequate excuse for why he was filled with so much rage, decade after decade, and chose to take it out on his family. But I had spent my lifetime wondering if it was possible to be *that kind of drunk* from alcoholism being an inherited tendency; suddenly learning about my father's traumatic past helped me better understand how he had become the man I knew. It was all, finally, starting to make sense. Sad, heartbreaking, shout-at-the-sky kind of sense.

I am left with sadness and a profound, futile wish. I wish my dad had decided to share his truth — with his family and friends, with law enforcement, with other community leaders — and seek help from a therapist well before he married my mom and had children. I know that's far easier said than done, especially all those years ago. I wonder how different things would be for me and Beth (and even for my mom) if he'd at least found it healing to reveal to me and Beth, in the last moments of his life, the unjust actions done to him. Deathbed admissions and final words can change an entire generation. Instead, he carried those demons into his marriage, his family, his job, and his community, and I suspect he blamed himself daily for what happened to him and who he had become.

Learning about my father's childhood abuse has been impactful and, in some ways, alters how I view my father's alcoholism — how I think about the ways he treated us and inflicted long-lasting trauma on my life. However, it does not give him a pass. I don't know what it's like to go through what he went through, but I'd like to think he could have eclipsed his wounds to have been a better man — that he could have given me and Beth a better childhood. I still believe he could've chosen to be a more loving, more invested, and more patient parent than the father he had — to be a father who opted for hugs and laughter over tobacco and beer. I am proud of the work I have done to choose differently — to end the cycles of abuse and addiction and family dysfunction. I always wished my dad had stopped the cycle during his generation instead of leaving all the healing to mine, but I accept that this is how it played out. I'm getting better at no longer asking so much "What if?"

As for me and my mom, I am happy to report that we have enjoyed some productive discussions since I wrote the manuscript of this book. She has expressed her intent to avoid reading the book (which may be for the best), and she has finally apologized for never previously acknowledging that she wasn't Rocky's only victim — that Beth and I suffered too. I'm working on acceptance and forgiveness, doing my best to meet her where she is (and knowing she may never go further).

Every step of my journey has helped me see that I am capable of so much. And I have discovered that what we've been through doesn't have to predict who we become. I am strong and resilient, capable of patience and affection, loving and loyal and devoted. If I can break the negative cycles perpetuated by my parents and grandparents, perhaps anyone can. My story is not unique, and that's why I've chosen to share it — to help others know they aren't alone, and to demonstrate the strength of the human spirit, regardless of where we come from or what our family dysfunction has looked like.

From the shadows of my past has emerged a profound empathy that guides me daily. My father's battles were not in vain; they sowed the seeds of resilience within me. And now, as a parent, I strive to provide a nurturing environment where my children can thrive, free from the shadows that once loomed over my own upbringing. Generation by generation, we're getting healthier instead of sicker — better instead of worse.

In the end, these experiences that I have laid bare in this book — burying my father and grieving for my uncle — have not just been acts of closure, but renewals of purpose. They are reminders that our past does not define us, but rather, it equips us with the tools to forge a better future. I hope that sharing my story offers solace to others who walk a similar path, and that it serves as a beacon of hope for those who, like me, have found strength in unexpected places.

For all the ground and miles covered in this book, I look forward to the many more car rides to come — the quiet time with myself and the beautiful, important time with the people I love, rocking out to good music and having conversations that break us wide open and put us back together again.

My Life in Pictures

2008 – Marshall, Michigan, July 4th Celebration: Kendall, Rocky & William

Cousins – William & Maddie Rayner with Kendall in their "boat" for the July 4th wagon parade

Rocky (29), Laurie (2), & Beth (3.5)

Laurie (3) & Beth (4) – "Best Buds"

Rocky carts Beth (l) & Laurie (r) to his beloved garden to gather vegetables to sell.

Trying to escape the madness inside the house, Mom crafted many backyard blanket forts – Laurie (5) & Beth (6).

1987 Jazz Duet - Beth & Laurie

1988 Jazz Solo
(When I believed I was fat)

1991 Lyrical Jazz Group, "Amazing Grace"

1992 & 1993 - Homecoming Dresses made by Miss Bobbi (Pictured here with me)

1980 - Laurie's 1st Recital, "Bathing Beauties"   September 1979 - Laurie's 1st Dance Class

1988 - Rocky's "King Tut" Recital Routine (Rocky is back row, far right.)

Brooks Memorial Fountain
Image by Michael Harding © 2021. www.miles2gobeforeIs-
leep.com. Used with permission.

Marshall Middle School
Image by Michael Harding © 2021. www.miles2gobeforeIs-
leep.com. Used with permission.

Downtown Marshall, MI
Image by Michael Harding © 2021. www.miles2gobeforeIsleep.com. Used with permission.

2022 – Josh, Skyler, & Kendall

Aimee Coury-Strand & Laurie – 1990

Rocky & Judy – engagement 1969

Sullivan Family: (L to R back row) Patti (19), Nancy (17), triplets Rocky, Mary. & Margie (15); (L to R front row) Mary Katherine, Jeanne (6), Dan (9) & Roger

Christmas 1978 - Rocky, Judy, Beth & Laurie

Easter Sunday 1977 - Judy (27),
Beth (3), Laurie (1.5)

Rocky's senior photo ("the Fonz") – 1966

Funeral for Rocky Sullivan – October 10, 2020. (L to R: Beth, Josh, Skyler, Laurie, & Kendall)

Proud "Dance Mom"

Beth & Laurie pay a visit to Rocky at The Riverside
– always smiling, acting as if all is "fine."

Acknowledgments

First and foremost, I am grateful to my children. To my courageous son, **Skyler Hellmann,** for constantly demonstrating that a diagnosis of autism does not equate to being broken or incapable of creating a tremendous impact on the world throughout his lifetime. And to my fiercely strong daughter, **Kendall Hurst,** whose gift of sarcasm and quick wit is balanced by her enormous heart and thoughtfulness for every living thing on this planet. Sis: Thank you for allowing me to tell YOUR story so significantly in this book and for being the best road-trip partner on the farewell tour for my dad.

People routinely tell me what a blessing my husband, **Josh Hellmann,** has been to our family, and I know that God placed that incredible man in my life exactly when I needed him. He has been unwavering in his faith and constantly encouraged me as I worked hard to restore mine. Equally as important, he listens to all my crazy ideas, loves me with every fiber of his being, and is an excellent role model to our children. Josh: You are my rock, my comedic equal, and my best friend.

During the early stages of my work on this book, I was fortunate to enlist the kindness of friends and family, each of whom enthusiastically agreed to review, edit, and provide feedback on my first draft. Most notably, my sister, **Beth Rayner**, who has an exceptional memory, not only went above and beyond to ensure my accuracy with specific dates and names but willingly revisited her own childhood traumas to assist me with the content of this book. She also never hesitated when I asked her to read and thoroughly edit every version (and there were many) of this manuscript. Her Master's in Reading degree really came in handy! Beth:

For my entire life, I have idolized your strength and feel forever blessed knowing you always have my back. Thank you for being a listening ear, saying yes, no matter what I ask of you and reminding me to be proud of myself.

My cousin and childhood bestie, **Courtney Burk**, eagerly accepted the task of reading my early drafts and provided the hugs I needed when the weight of the stories left us both heartbroken. Courtney: You inspire me to be my authentic self — which means never apologizing for sneaking into the kitchen at midnight to eat the brownies!

My dear friend, **Feef Dillon**, who first welcomed middle-school- aged me into her family as a babysitter for her sons, quickly became both a second mother and mentor for most of my life. Feef: Your feedback and support throughout every stage of writing this emotional book meant the absolute world to me. Thank you for your never-ending love and guidance and for having a very active social life so I could escape to your beautiful, stress-free home to watch Keegan and Remy.

Growing up in a small town that housed one middle school and one high school made it easy to develop extremely close friendships, many of which I have been blessed to maintain into adulthood. I am eternally grateful for the youthful memories made from sleepovers, innocent she-nanigans around town, and countless hours spent talking about boys and playing sports with **Nicole Segee-Gluck, Aimee Coury-Strand, Summer Shubert-Gilmer, Lauren O'Dowd-Nienhuis, Nancy Kennedy-Chap-man, Mary Carlton,** and **Carrie Purucker-Blanck.** Girls: Thanks for all the laughter and fun times that provided much calm to my storm.

To my Bobbi's Dance Studio competition team sisters — **Kristin Ra-mos-Keyes, Carrie Grable-McAdam** (who was also my ride-or-die bestie)**, Lori Abbott-Robertson, Leslie Denbrock-Bennett, Amy Young-Her-guth,** and **Jennifer Whitesell-Norder** — thank you for helping me feel normal and a part of something uplifting and important. When we took the stage together as a tight family unit, the negativity drilled into my head was silenced and I finally had a reason to smile. I loved every second spent dancing and making fond memories with each of you.

Thank you to my **Aunt Nancy Hood, Aunt Jeanne Sullivan,** and **Uncle Dan (Mickey) Sullivan** for your willingness to travel back to some of the challenging times in your childhood home to share with me those untold stories of Rocky Sullivan's young life. I've learned so much more about my dad, the person I never truly knew, and I appreciate and love each of you dearly for your encouragement and understanding as I tell my story.

I am so grateful to the amazing individuals who wrote endorsements for my book: **Carrie Cariello, Kate Colbert, Shannon Urquiola, Allison Luallen, Sandy Lamb, Dawnmarie Gaivin, Laura Leaton Roberts, Joanna Monahan, Candice Putnam, Sue Rosko, Karen Roberts, Feef Dillon,** and **Max Peel.**

Special thanks to my talented friend, **Anna May,** of Anna May Photography for capturing the perfect professional headshots and marketing photos utilized for this book launch.

Go Beyond the Book
and
Keep in Touch with Laurie L. Hellmann

In addition to hosting a podcast for several years and being complimented for her conversational style that makes guests extremely comfortable, Laurie L. Hellmann's messages, experiences, and insights have been called inspirational and powerful. She is a storyteller in every way. Laurie openly shares her honest, personal journey from childhood to parenthood and provides an educational component while igniting hope in others. But most of all, she is relatable and helps each person feel seen. Laurie believes that when we invite others to better understand the paths we are walking, we are better able to join hands and walk together with purpose.

Through her compassion, humor, and desire to educate the world on the importance of personal growth and living your best life, Laurie motivates audiences to gain a renewed perspective and take action.

Hire Laurie to:

- Inspire your team, organization, or audience with storytelling.
- Deliver a powerful and motivational keynote address to audiences of all sizes on topics including perspective, resiliency, inclusion, mental health, and belief in a higher purpose.
- Facilitate workshops and lead panel discussions.
- Read from her book and host book signings.

KEEP IN TOUCH

Listen to the podcast – Living the Sky Life:

(Apple) https://podcasts.apple.com/us/podcast/
living-the-sky-life-autism-journey/id1480273037

(Spotify) https://open.spotify.com/show/01hMzt5cwvyJgZJtXcKGHH

(Google Play) https://play.google.com/music/listen?u=0#/ps/
Igma3jgyi3nib2i5ht7h2yzccwm

(Audible) https://a.co/d/5NVvDqK

Send an email:

Laurie@LaurieHellmann.com

Find, follow and share on social media:

in Linkedin.com/in/Laurie-Hellmann-1a2ba410/

f Facebook.com/WelcomeToMyAutismLife

○ Instagram.com/WelcomeToMyLife_LaurieHellmann/

Selling Vegetables to Drunks is Book #2 in the
Purposeful Journey Series. Book #1, *Welcome to My Life: A Personal Parenting
Journey Through Autism*, is available everywhere books are sold.

About the Author

Laurie L. Hellmann is originally from Marshall, Michigan, and moved to Southern Indiana following graduation from Ball State University in 1997. Laurie earned her Bachelor of Science degree in Legal Administration from BSU, an MBA from Indiana University Southeast, and has enjoyed a successful, 25-year professional career in the healthcare industry.

Throughout her entire life, Laurie has assumed the role of caregiver, but it was through her 21 years (and counting) of experience parenting a child with profound needs that she discovered the true purpose for her life — to serve as an advocate and beacon of hope for those who feel lost or broken.

Laurie authored her first book, *Welcome to My Life: A Personal Parenting Journey Through Autism*, in 2020 and is excited to bring you, *Selling Vegetables to Drunks*, the second book in her memoir series.

Through her writing, her podcast (*Living the Sky Life – Our Autism Journey*), her advocacy work and her speaking events — all centered around resiliency, perspective, and belief in a higher purpose — Laurie is continually striving to make a lasting impact in the autism community and beyond.

Made in the USA
Middletown, DE
09 September 2024